TREKKING IN THE VANOISE

TOUR OF THE VANOISE AND THE TOUR DES GLACIERS DE LA VANOISE

by Kev Reynolds and Jonathan Williams

JUNIPER HOUSE, MURLEY MOSS,
OXENHOLME ROAD, KENDAL, CUMBRIA LA9 7RL
www.cicerone.co.uk

© Kev Reynolds and Jonathan Williams 2021
Third edition 2021
ISBN: 978 1 85284 863 7
Second edition 2009
First edition 1996

Printed by Severn, Gloucester, on responsibly sourced paper
A catalogue record for this book is available from the British Library.
All photographs are by the author unless otherwise stated.

Route mapping by Lovell Johns www.lovelljohns.com
Contains OpenStreetMap.org data © OpenStreetMap
contributors, CC-BY-SA. NASA relief data courtesy of ESRI

The routes of the GR®, PR® and GRP® paths in this
guide have been reproduced with the permission of the
Fédération Française de la Randonnée Pédestre holder of the exclusive rights of
the routes. The names GR®, PR® and GRP® are registered trademarks. © FFRP
2021 for all GR®, PR® and GRP® paths appearing in this work.

Updates to this guide

While every effort is made by our authors to ensure the accuracy of guidebooks as
they go to print, changes can occur during the lifetime of an edition. This guidebook was researched and written before and during the COVID-19 pandemic.
While we are not aware of any significant changes to routes or facilities at the
time of printing, it is likely that the current situation will give rise to more changes
than would usually be expected. Any updates that we know of for this guide will
be on the Cicerone website (www.cicerone.co.uk/863/updates), so please check
before planning your trip. We also advise that you check information about such
things as transport, accommodation and shops locally. Even rights of way can be
altered over time.

We are always grateful for information about any discrepancies between
a guidebook and the facts on the ground, sent by email to updates@cicerone.
co.uk or by post to Cicerone, Juniper House, Murley Moss, Oxenholme Road,
Kendal, LA9 7RL.

Register your book: To sign up to receive free updates, special offers and
GPX files where available, register your book at www.cicerone.co.uk.

Front cover: The Grande Casse dominates the northern sections of the Vanoise
National Park

CONTENTS

Map key

    ⟁   hotel/accommodation

    ⊕   restaurant

    ⊕   supermarket/grocery store

    ⊞   ATM

    🚉   rail station

    🚌   bus station

    𝒊   tourist information

    ▲   manned hut

    🅿   parking

    ⌂   unmanned hut

Note on mapping

The route maps in this guide are derived from publicly available data, databases and crowd-sourced data. As such, they have not been through the detailed checking procedures that would generally be applied to a published map from an official mapping agency. However, we have reviewed them closely in the light of local knowledge as part of the preparation of this guide.

ACKNOWLEDGEMENTS

The first two editions of this guide concentrated on the Tour of the Vanoise and were published under my name; Jonathan Williams has now added more multi-day routes in order to create this present volume, which we've renamed *Trekking in the Vanoise* to reflect the region's wider appeal. This title, then, is very much a joint effort. My thanks as ever go to Jonathan and all at Cicerone for bringing it together, to my wife Min, and friends John and Janette Robertson for their company on some of the treks, and to the numerous refuge *gardiens* who provide welcome hospitality and advice whenever sought. The Vanoise National Park is a trekker's delight and it deserves to be better known among English-speaking enthusiasts. Hopefully this guide will help you enjoy as many rewarding days of activity there as we did while researching the various routes described.

Once again, I am reminded that the production of a guidebook is a team effort calling on the skills, talents and dedication of many people. It may be the author's name on the cover, but cartographer, designer, editor, printer and binder clothe the bare skeleton of words and give it true value. My sincere thanks to all involved in the production of this guidebook, and to you for buying it.

Kev Reynolds

After ten days' trekking, the Aiguille Doran and peaks above Modane are seen once more on the final stage of the ToV

Mountain safety

Every mountain walk has its dangers, and those described in this guidebook are no exception. All who walk or climb in the mountains should recognise this and take responsibility for themselves and their companions along the way. The author and publisher have made every effort to ensure that the information contained in this guide was correct when it went to press, but, except for any liability that cannot be excluded by law, they cannot accept responsibility for any loss, injury or inconvenience sustained by any person using this book.

International distress signal *(emergency only)*
Six blasts on a whistle (and flashes with a torch after dark) spaced evenly for one minute, followed by a minute's pause. Repeat until an answer is received. The response is three signals per minute followed by a minute's pause.

Helicopter rescue
The following signals are used to communicate with a helicopter:

Help needed:
raise both arms
above head to
form a 'Y'

Help not needed:
raise one arm
above head, extend
other arm downward

Emergency telephone numbers
If telephoning from the UK the dialling code for France is 0033
Emergency services: tel 112
PGHM (Peloton de Gendarmerie de Haute Montagne, mountain rescue):
tel 04 79 05 18 04 (Modane)
tel 04 79 07 01 10 (Bourg-St-Maurice)

Weather reports
https://meteofrance.com tel 3250
Or use your preferred mountain weather app.

Mountain rescue can be very expensive – be adequately insured.

ROUTE SUMMARY TABLES

Tour of the Vanoise

Stage	Start	Finish	Distance (km)	Ascent (m)	Descent (m)	Walking time	Page
1	Modane	Refuge de l'Orgère	6	890	negligible	3hr	41
2	Refuge de l'Orgère	Refuge de Plan Sec	13	870	490	5hr	46
3	Refuge de Plan Sec	Refuge de l'Arpont	16	750	760	5hr 30min	52
4	Refuge de l'Arpont	Refuge du Plan du Lac	13.5	730	680	4hr 30min	58
5	Refuge du Plan du Lac	Refuge du Vallonbrun	18.5	720	810	6hr 30min	64
6	Refuge du Vallonbrun	Bonneval-sur-Arc	16	180	640	4hr 30min	71
7	Bonneval-sur-Arc	Val d'Isère	14.5	980	980	5hr 30min	79
8	Val d'Isère	Refuge de la Leisse	18.5	1190	500	7hr	94
9	Refuge de la Leisse	Pralognan-la-Vanoise	18	450	1520	6hr	108
10	Pralognan-la-Vanoise	Refuge de Péclet-Polset	14	1080	30	5hr	120
11	Refuge de Péclet-Polset	Modane	15	360	1790	5hr 30min	126
Total			**163**	**8200**	**8200**	**11 days (58hr)**	

Variants and alternatives

Stage	Start	Finish	Distance (km)	Ascent (m)	Descent (m)	Walking time	Page
7: variant via Col des Fours	Bonneval-sur-Arc	Val d'Isère	18	1200	1200	6hr 30min	86
8: variant via the Tovière	Val d'Isère	Refuge de la Leisse	17	1230	550	7hr	101

Stage	Start	Finish	Distance (km)	Ascent (m)	Descent (m)	Walking time	Page
7A	Bonneval-sur-Arc	Refuge de la Femma	20	1610	1070	8hr	89
8A	Val d'Isère	Refuge de la Femma	18	1290	750	7hr	103
9A	Refuge de la Femma	Pralognan-la-Vanoise	23	540	1470	7hr	117

Stage	Start	Finish	Distance (km)	Ascent (m)	Descent (m)	Walking time	Page
Tour des Glaciers de la Vanoise							
1	Pralognan-la-Vanoise	Refuge de la Valette	10	1550	420	5hr	136
2	Refuge de la Valette	Refuge du Fond d'Aussois	20	1230	1450	8hr	140
3	Refuge du Fond d'Aussois	Refuge de l'Arpont	20	860	880	6hr 30min	145
4	Refuge de l'Arpont	Refuge du Col de la Vanoise	14	660	450	5hr	149
5	Refuge du Col de la Vanoise	Pralognan-la-Vanoise	8	negligible	1100	2hr 30min	152
Totals			**72**	**4300**	**4300**	**5 days (27hr)**	

Stage	Start	Finish	Distance (km)	Ascent (m)	Descent (m)	Walking time	Page
Tour of the Eastern Vanoise							
1	Bonneval-sur-Arc	Refuge du Vallonbrun	16	640	180	5hr	158
2	Refuge du Vallonbrun	Refuge du Plan du Lac	18.5	810	720	6hr	160

Stage	Start	Finish	Distance (km)	Ascent (m)	Descent (m)	Walking time	Page
3	Refuge du Plan du Lac	Refuge du Fond des Fours	18	770	590	6hr	160
4	Refuge du Fond des Fours	Bonneval-sur-Arc	11.5	460	1190	4hr	161
Totals			**64**	**2680**	**2680**	**4 days (21hr)**	

Tour of the Western Vanoise

Stage	Start	Finish	Distance (km)	Ascent (m)	Descent (m)	Walking time	Page
1	Pralognan-la-Vanoise	Refuge de Péclet-Polset	14	1080	30	5hr	162
2	Refuge de Péclet-Polset	Refuge des Lacs Merlet	15	950	1030	6hr	162
3	Refuge des Lacs Merlet	Pralognan-la-Vanoise	19	440	1410	6hr	164
Totals			**48**	**2470**	**2470**	**3 days (17hr)**	

Traverse of the Vanoise via the GR5 and GR55

Stage	Start	Finish	Distance (km)	Ascent (m)	Descent (m)	Walking time	Page
1	Landry	Refuge d'Entre-le-Lac	18	1580	200	6hr 30min	166
2	Refuge d'Entre-le-Lac	Refuge de la Leisse	21	1170	830	7hr	168
3	Refuge de la Leisse	Pralognan-la-Vanoise	18	450	1520	6hr	169
4	Pralognan-la-Vanoise	Refuge de Péclet-Polset	14	1080	30	5hr	169
5	Refuge de Péclet-Polset	Modane	15	360	1790	5hr 30min	169
Totals			**86**	**4640**	**4370**	**5 days (30hr)**	

The Refuge de l'Orgère is nearly 1000m above Modane and there are views to the mountains of the south, including the Écrins massif (ToV, Stage 1)

Climbing towards the Col du Grand Marchet (TdGV, Stage 1)

INTRODUCTION

The trail after the Refuge de l'Arpont (TdGV, Stage 4)

This book is a guide to trekking in one of the most attractive mountain regions in France. The main route described is the 10–12-day Tour of the Vanoise (ToV), but the popular week-long Tour des Glaciers de la Vanoise (TdGV) is also included, as are three shorter tours in the same area, all of which amount to a summer's worth of activity in a sublime setting.

Located in Savoie, between Mont Blanc and the Massif des Écrins, southeast of Chambéry and close to the Italian border, the Vanoise Alps contain more than 100 summits in excess of 3000m. These are the quintessential Alps, whose major peaks are daubed with shrinking glaciers and snowfields and whose valleys glisten with lakes, streams and waterfalls. There are towering moraine walls, impossibly steep rock slabs and, in the early summer, meadows extravagant with a riot of Alpine flowers. Almost every district has its old stone ruins, deserted chapels, isolated farms and tiny hamlets that seem to belong to a long-forgotten age. There's a wonderland of marked trails to explore, scenic cols to cross, a variety of mountain huts in which to spend the night and abundant wildlife to enrich each day.

Trekking in the Vanoise is the perfect way to experience some of the finest walking in the Alps without being encumbered by rope or ice axe.

TOUR OF THE VANOISE

Making what could be described as a figure-of-eight trek in and around the very best of the Vanoise National Park, the main Tour of the Vanoise should appeal to all keen mountain walkers. Totalling a distance of more than 160km through a series of dramatic wild landscapes, it is demanding in places and, with several passes to tackle in excess of 2500m, the total ascent amounts to some 8200m. Each stage has its challenge and its rewards. But there are no glacier crossings, no difficult or prolonged scrambling and no lengthy sections of path exposed to either stonefall or vertigo-inducing exposure. Waymarks and cairns are usually clear enough where the trail is indistinct, and in places signposts have been erected to give a rough indication of the time required to reach the next hut, col or village along the way.

The route is an obvious one. The southern section of that classic long-distance trail, the GR5, runs from Lake Geneva to the Mediterranean, and by combining this with the GR55, which cuts through the wild heart of the region, a multi-day tour becomes a practical reality. Although not as well known as the Tour of Mont Blanc, nor as challenging as the Tour of the Oisans, the Tour of the Vanoise is every bit as inspiring and rewarding as these two neighbouring routes. It is an undoubted classic, and one which offers a perfect introduction to Alpine hut-to-hut trekking.

TOUR DES GLACIERS DE LA VANOISE

The five-day Tour des Glaciers de la Vanoise forms a roughly oval-shaped circuit around the spectacular central group of high mountains located between the Arc valley to the south, the Doron depths to the east and the Pralognan valley to the west. Partly sharing its route with the Tour of the Vanoise and staying continuously high, it takes in some of the highest cols in the region and can include an optional easy 3000m peak, the Pointe de l'Observatoire. Just under 75km long and with 4300m of ascent, it

fits comfortably into a one-week trip for those who might not have time to manage the full Tour of the Vanoise.

Tour of the Eastern Vanoise (Tour de Méan Martin et du Grand Roc Noir)

Close to the northeastern limit of the Vanoise National Park, the Pointe de Méan Martin and the Grand Roc Noir are high points on a long ridge of 3000m peaks that wall the Haute-Maurienne. This tour makes an elongated circuit of that wall over four days, using three national park refuges for accommodation. Two passes in excess of 2900m have to be crossed, and since they are both likely to have snow cover until late June at the earliest, walkers are advised not to attempt the route too early in the season. The trek begins and ends at the attractive village of Bonneval-sur-Arc.

Tour of the Western Vanoise

This three-day tour of the western section of the national park follows the route of the Tour of the Vanoise from Pralognan-la-Vanoise to the Refuge de Péclet-Polset, then explores little-known country to the north. After passing Lac Blanc and the high point of the tour at the remote Col du Soufre, it makes a long descent beside the Gébroulaz glacier to the Refuge du Saut, before again striking into seldom-walked terrain on its way to a traditional refuge at the beautiful Lacs Merlet. The last day takes in a high viewpoint before dropping back down into the Pralognan valley, where a fourth day could easily be spent if desired.

Traverse of the Vanoise via the GR5 and GR55

By combining the GR5 with the GR55, this splendid north-to-south crossing of the district can be achieved in five days. A linear route (rather than a circular tour), it forms one of the highlights of the 674km Grande Traversée des Alpes, the full extent of which will take most walkers at least four weeks to complete. Beginning in Landry in the lower Isère valley, the first day

Mountains rise south of the Arc valley (ToV, Stage 2)

follows the GR5, passing a string of villages to reach more remote countryside on the edge of the national park. After crossing Col du Palet, the way drops to Tignes le Lac, from where the traverse then heads south to join the GR55, now following Stages 9–11 of the scenic Tour of the Vanoise all the way to Modane.

An optional alternative is available below Refuge de la Leisse, where the GR5 heads south along the Doron's valley, effectively reversing the first few stages of the Tour of the Vanoise to reach Modane.

THE VANOISE NATIONAL PARK

Located between the upper valleys of the Isère (Tarentaise) and Arc (Maurienne) in the *département* of Savoie, and adjoining Italy's Gran Paradiso National Park along a 14km boundary, the Parc National de la Vanoise (PNV) was established in 1963, largely to protect the dwindling population of *bouquetin* (ibex), and was the first to come into existence in France. The PNV and the Gran Paradiso National Park were twinned in 1972, and together they now constitute the largest nature reserve in Western Europe.

The PNV covers an area of 53,000ha (205 square miles) of high mountains and deep, verdant valleys, ranging in altitude from 1280m to 3855m. With 107 peaks over 3000m, numerous glaciers (now retreating fast) and a network of around 500km of footpaths – many of which are snow-free from mid June to late October – the broader park area contains around 60 refuges, of which 17 belong to the PNV authority. The rest either belong to the Fédération Française des Clubs Alpins et de Montagne (FFCAM; formerly the Club Alpin Français, CAF) or are in private ownership.

RESPONSIBLE TREKKING

- Keep to footpaths – don't take shortcuts, which can lead to erosion.
- Don't pick or uproot plants, and avoid trampling delicate vegetation when taking photographs.
- Don't make unnecessary noise.
- Dogs are not allowed, even on a leash.
- Respect wildlife and livestock.
- Don't leave litter. Take your rubbish away with you for proper disposal.
- Offsite camping is restricted to the vicinity of specified refuges.
- Don't light fires.
- Hang-gliding is banned to avoid disturbing wildlife and livestock.
- Mountain biking is forbidden to avoid path erosion.

While tourist development – especially downhill skiing – has been encouraged on the park's periphery, the central zone is protected from outside exploitation, and, despite a small number of summer farms, there's no permanent habitation. As a result, the park boasts an abundance of wildlife and some of the most spectacular displays of Alpine flowers in all Europe: see 'Wildlife and Alpine flowers' below. (For further reading material about the Vanoise and neighbouring regions, see Appendix D.)

There are, of course, rules governing visitors to the national park – see 'Responsible trekking'. But it's a walker's paradise, and the various tours suggested here explore a number of its finest valleys.

Young bouquetin *perched above the Doron de Termignon*

WILDLIFE AND ALPINE FLOWERS

Animals

The creation of the national park has been beneficial to wildlife in general, and the *bouquetin* (ibex) in particular, whose population within the park has risen to around 2000. This number represents a third of all *bouquetin* in Alpine France, and you would be extremely unlucky (or unobservant) not to enjoy several sightings of these handsome creatures on any of the treks described here.

In the late 19th century, the *bouquetin* had disappeared from almost every part of the European Alps, with the exception of the Gran Paradiso in Italy where it was saved from total extinction by Victor Emmanuel II, whose royal hunting grounds were turned into a national park in 1922.

Gradually, small herds were rein-
troduced to other Alpine regions,
including the neighbouring Vanoise
district, and it is from that original
stock that the present population has
developed.

Short-legged and stocky, *bouquetin* live and graze in herds, the sexes
mostly remaining apart until the rut,
when one dominant buck will win a
harem of females. The male sports a
large pair of knobbly scimitar-shaped
horns, which are used in battle with
rival males during the autumn rut. The
female's horns are much shorter and
her body less stocky than her male
counterpart's. Although they are normally shy of human contact, within
the national park it is sometimes possible to study groups – grazing or simply at rest – at close quarters.

The chamois is also frequently
observed grazing in small herds
away from habitation and is easily
distinguished from the *bouquetin*
by its short curved horns, distinctive
white lower jaw and dark reddish-
brown coat with a black stripe along
its spine. A member of the antelope
family and virtually a symbol of the
Alps, there are some 5500 within
the national park. The chamois is
extremely agile, has an incomparable
sense of smell and acute hearing, and
makes a sharp wheezing sound when
disturbed.

The marmot is the most endear-
ing and commonly seen of all Alpine
creatures. Living in colonies among
sheltering rocks, as well as in more
open pasturelands below the snow-
line, this large rodent grows to the
size of a hare and can weigh as much
as 10kg. It spends five to six months
each winter in hibernation in an
underground burrow, emerging in late
springtime looking scrawny and lean.
Feeding on the rich summer grasses
soon builds up reserves of fat in both
adult and young cub alike.

The marmot needs to be vigilant,
for predators such as fox and eagle
can strike at any time. A shrill warning cry emitted from the back of the
throat, rather like a bird's whistle, is
the alarm that sends it scurrying for
cover. There should be opportunities
to observe marmots on all the routes
in this guide.

The small but lively stoat is
another inhabitant of the upper pasturelands. This streamlined long-tailed
carnivore preys on ground-nesting
birds but will also attack animals
much bigger than itself – mountain
hare, for example, or a young marmot. In the summer months, the
stoat's fur is a russet fawn with white
throat and underbelly, but in winter
it turns completely white to merge
with the snowfields. If you're lucky,
you may see one sunning itself among
rocks beside the trail or running along
a low drystone wall.

A little smaller and not so long
in the body as the stoat, the weasel
is also on the list of mammals to be
found within the national park, along
with fox, badger and pine marten, the
latter inhabiting the coniferous forests

that clothe the surrounding valleys. Although it consumes vast quantities of berries, the pine marten preys largely on the red squirrel, which it pursues from tree to tree.

Birds

In the same forests, the nutcracker is perhaps more often heard than seen, for it rivals the jay as the policeman of the woods with its raucous warning call of 'kre-kre-kre'. With its large head, strong beak, tawny speckled breast and swooping flight, the nutcracker is noted for the way it breaks open pinecones to access the fatty seeds, which it then stores away to feed on in winter.

The nutcracker is just one of 120 bird species nesting in the Vanoise region: others include the wall creeper, pied flycatcher, crossbill, rock thrush and the rare three-toed woodpecker. About 20 pairs of golden eagles have been recorded, and the bearded vulture, or lammergeier,

is making a comeback, thanks to a repopulation programme which began in 1986.

The bearded vulture is a true colossus, its wingspan measuring almost 3m, its large body and powerful neck culminating in a pale head with a black band that extends from piercing eye to curved beak. It feeds largely on the bones of sheep or cattle, from which it extracts marrow by dropping the bones onto rocks from a great height.

Flowers

As for mountain flowers, more than 1000 species have been recorded growing above 1300m – not only Alpine natives but southern and oriental species too, and Arctic flowers left behind by previous ice ages. Walking the trails described in this guidebook, you will be reminded daily of the richness of this flora. Although seasons vary from one year to the next, the most extensive displays will most likely be found from late June to mid July, when every level – from deep

Moss campion; yellow mountain saxifrage

valley to high pass – will be extravagant with colour.

The south-facing slopes of the Crête de la Turra (west of Refuge du Cuchet), and the valley meadows between Col de la Madeleine (below Refuge du Vallonbrun) and Bonneval, are among the most lavish in all the Vanoise. Go there in early summer and you'll be wading through carpets of orchid, polygonum, dianthus, larkspur and vetch. There'll be cowslip, marsh marigold, potentilla and yellow archangel, pink cranesbill and rock rose, vivid blue campanula, violas in assorted varieties and masses of clover thick with bees.

On sunny hillsides around 2000m, the delicate white blooms of St Bruno's lily (*Paradisea liliastrum*) will be seen in huge swathes, their several heads, on a long stem, all facing the same way. On other hillsides it might be the hairy-stemmed spring anemone (*Pulsatilla vernalis*) that dominates, or maybe its cousin, the white Alpine anemone (*Pulsatilla alpina*).

In the shade of woods, on open pastures and among marshy areas, the great yellow gentian (*Gentiana lutea*) – which looks nothing like either of the better-known spring or trumpet gentians – produces numerous flower-clusters on an erect stalk which can be more than a metre tall. The almost stemless spring gentian (*Gentiana verna*) appears all over the Vanoise, as does the aptly named trumpet gentian (*Gentiana kochiana*), often found

among soft pink primula. Those harbingers of spring, the tassel-headed snowbells (*Soldanella*), cannot wait for summer and will often be found blooming in the midst of a patch of melting snow.

Alpenroses form a great splash of scarlet on hillsides and in valleys throughout the district, with one of the finest displays just above Pont de Croé-Vie on the eastern approach to Col de la Vanoise. Much smaller than the alpenrose, spreading as bright cushions on rocks, are assorted species of saxifrage and rock jasmine (*Androsace*), while the common houseleek (*Sempervivum tectorum*) sprouts luxuriant flower stems in July from a fleshy rosette anchored to a wayside boulder.

Several of the refuges visited on these treks have copies of a beautifully illustrated book that identifies the flora of the region. If you're interested in mountain flowers, ask to borrow a copy to browse during your stay.

WHEN TO GO

The region receives plenty of snowfall in winter – hence the siting of some of France's most popular ski slopes on the outer fringe of the national park. The disappearance of this snow from the high cols determines the best time to tackle any of the treks in this book, and although it may be possible to cross some of the passes as early as mid June following a particularly mild winter, the beginning of July is usually early enough – and even then some of the cols and north- (or east-) facing slopes can have their troublesome sections.

The first two weeks of July in a 'normal' season will see Alpine flowers at their best, when the lower meadows, as yet uncut, reward the trekker with an extravagant display of colour and fragrance, forming one of the highlights of the Vanoise district.

French holidays extend between mid July and mid August, and, as huts are likely to be crowded during this period (and, in extreme cases, fully booked), accommodation can be difficult to find unless pre-booked. August can be very warm. Protected from oceanic rains by the Pre-Alps, the Vanoise enjoys a dry sunny climate, almost Mediterranean in its intensity.

September offers perhaps the most favourable conditions for a trekking holiday here. Gone are the crowds, summer's heat is beginning to wane and prolonged periods of settled weather are often to be had. Days are drawing in, of course, but there should still be plenty of daylight in which to complete each stage. Although the best of the flowers will be over, the meadows and grassy hillsides still produce occasional gems.

HOW TO GET THERE

The main Tour of the Vanoise and the shorter Tour of the Eastern Vanoise are both accessed via Modane, while the Tour des Glaciers de la Vanoise and the Tour of the Western Vanoise begin at Pralognan-la-Vanoise. The linear Traverse of the Vanoise via the GR5 and GR55 starts at Landry.

By air

The nearest international airports for the Vanoise region are at Turin (1hr 30min from Modane by train), Chambéry (1hr 30min), Lyon St Exupéry (2hr), Grenoble (2hr 30min) and Geneva (2hr 30min), all of which have rail links with Modane via Chambéry. For access to Pralognan, the easiest options are Geneva and Lyon; there is no approach from Turin.

As flight routings and schedules are notoriously vulnerable to change, you are advised to check the current situation online. Contact details for airlines and comparison websites are given in Appendix A.

By rail

The fastest approach by rail from the UK is via the high-speed Eurostar from London St Pancras to Paris (Gare du Nord) in 3hr, followed by the Paris (Gare de Lyon) to Turin high-speed TGV service, which stops at Modane, taking about 4hr from Paris.

To reach Pralognan, take the train to Chambéry then transfer to the Bourg-St-Maurice line and stop at Moûtiers. In summer, buses run from Moûtiers station up to Pralognan; out of season, a taxi will be necessary. Landry railway station lies between Chambéry and Bourg-St-Maurice.

Bonneval-sur-Arc lies at the end of a flat grassy valley (ToV, Stage 6)

For rail journeys within Europe, visit www.thetrainline.com or www.raileurope.com. To check timetables for French trains, go to www.sncf.com/fr. For general information on European rail travel, see www.seat61.com.

By car

Both Pralognan and Modane can be approached on the French motorway system, although parking would need to be pre-arranged via your hotel.

ACCOMMODATION

Overnight accommodation on each of the treks described in this guide will primarily be in mountain refuges, while hotels or *gîtes d'étape* (walkers' hostels) are the main options in valley resorts and villages. Although there are usually sufficient beds available, the demand will be high during July and August, when advance booking is essential to ensure a place. Out of the high season but before the refuges close for the winter, unless you're planning to trek with a group, a phone call made one day in advance is often sufficient, and the hut *gardien* (warden) will usually do this for you. Refuge telephone numbers and websites (where available) are given in this guide – see Appendix B. It is also possible to book beds in national park refuges online by going to www.refuges-vanoise.com.

Hotels: Accommodation in valley resorts and villages will usually be found in a limited number of hotels, which mostly hold a one- or two-star rating or are ungraded. Rooms with en-suite facilities are the norm, although some lower-priced options may have shared toilets in a corridor. When checking in, enquire whether breakfast (*petit déjeuner*) is included in the room price.

Gîtes d'étape: These are similar to private youth hostels and are geared to the needs of outdoor enthusiasts. As in mountain refuges (see below), sleeping accommodation is invariably in mixed-sex communal dormitories. Hot showers are almost always available and meals will be provided. Most *gîtes* also have self-catering facilities.

Camping: Although backpacking is possible, since the majority of the routes lie within the national park, offsite camping is forbidden and restrictions are enforced. However, for a small fee, an overnight pitch is currently allowed between 1 July and 31 August in designated areas near several refuges. Any such provisions are mentioned in the route description. Official campsites can be found in the surrounding valleys at Modane, Bessans, Val d'Isère and Pralognan-la-Vanoise.

Refuges: As mentioned above, refuges (or mountain huts, as they're often known) are the main form of overnight accommodation. Most of these are owned by the national park authority (the PNV), but some belong to the Fédération Française des Clubs Alpins et de Montagne (FFCAM), formerly the Club Alpin Français (CAF); the rest are privately owned but open to all. They are usually manned by a *gardien* from early/mid June until late September. Note that restrictions placed on visitor numbers and use of refuges during the COVID-19 period may continue for some time.

In the mixed-sex dormitories, each bed-space is allocated two blankets (or a duvet) and a pillow, but in the interests of hygiene visitors are expected to provide their own sleeping bag liner. Communal washrooms are standard (the majority have hot showers).

Meals are provided in all refuges where there is a resident *gardien*; *demi-pension* (bed, breakfast and evening meal) is available at almost every refuge used on the tours. The only refuge where there is no *gardien* is the Refuge du Cuchet, but note that in 2021 the Chalet-Refuge Bonneval-sur-Arc was open with restricted numbers and was at times unmanned due to COVID-19 restrictions; both are on the Tour of the Vanoise and the Tour of the Eastern Vanoise. All other refuges have *gardiens* in residence for the summer, although it is best to check in advance with the Refuge des Lacs Merlet (Tour of the Western Vanoise) as it is very small.

Evening meals invariably consist of three or more courses, often with several helpings of soup and bread available. A simple meat course served with potatoes, rice or pasta is often followed by a green salad, then cheese or a choice of dessert. Vegetarians are catered for if requested when booking in. Wine, beer and soft drinks are usually available. Breakfasts are 'continental style'

– plenty of bread and jam (sometimes cheese) and in some cases cereals are also on offer. A choice of coffee, tea or hot chocolate will usually be provided with breakfast. Lunch packets (*pique-niques*) can be arranged, while a few snack items to take away with you are often stocked by the *gardien*. Refuges usually offer light meals, snacks and drinks during the day.

Except for privately owned refuges, the majority of huts have a winter room that is permanently open, where walkers have the use of a kitchen, sleeping room and toilet. This is particularly useful during those times of year when there is no resident *gardien* and the main part of the hut is locked. Note that the water supply is often turned off during winter to avoid frozen pipes so you will have to source water elsewhere.

Hut conventions

To book a place in a mountain refuge, phone in advance. Telephone numbers are given throughout the route descriptions, and websites are listed in Appendix B.

On arrival at the hut, remove boots and leave them (with your trekking poles) in the porch or boot room, and select a pair of special hut shoes, usually provided for indoor wear. Locate the *gardien* to inform them of your arrival, and book whatever meals you require.

When you've been allocated bedspace, go to the dormitory and make your bed using the sleeping bag liner you have brought. Keep a head torch handy, as the room may not be lit after dark.

As mentioned above, snacks and drinks are usually available during

Refuge de la Femma, a welcome sight at the end of a long day (ToV, Stages 7A and 8A)

the day, but dinner and breakfast are served at set times. When the hut is busy, you will probably be allocated a specific place at the table.

Some *gardiens* require payment the night before you leave. Make sure you have sufficient cash to cover all your needs, as credit cards are not always accepted in huts.

NOTES FOR WALKERS

Although the routes described in this guide make multi-day journeys through a high Alpine environment, no technical skills are demanded of the trekker. However, there are a few very brief exposed sections – usually safeguarded by a fixed cable handrail

PNV waymarking: signposting; turn right; straight ahead

– that could be unnerving for those unused to precipitous slopes, and in such instances extra caution may be required.

Under normal summer conditions the trails should be clear of snow and ice, but sometimes unbridged streams flow across them. In such cases you'll need to find a way to cross, either by use of semi-submerged rocks or by simply wading through. Again, caution is advised.

Since most of the tours described have adopted lengthy sections of both the GR5 and GR55, the standard waymark to look for is a red-and-white horizontal stripe painted on trees, rocks or buildings. In some places, locally sponsored routes have additional coloured stripes. These are unlikely to cause confusion, however, and the route descriptions in

this book should keep you on course. The majority of trail junctions will be marked with a signpost, often quoting the approximate amount of time needed to reach the next refuge, village or notable feature.

Since the frequency of accommodation and provision of meals makes backpacking unnecessary, a light rucksack containing only the essentials for a two-week walking tour should leave you free to enjoy the experience without being burdened with camping gear. A list of suggested equipment is given below. Get yourself fit before you start, for there are plenty of steep inclines and several fairly long stages, which will be easier to tackle if you've made an effort to get in shape before leaving home. You'll not regret it.

When trekking, be considerate if making a toilet stop during the day. Keep well away from water sources, burn used toilet paper and bury faeces as effectively as possible. Remote buildings or ruins should not be used as public conveniences; they could serve as an emergency shelter – not only for other walkers, but for yourself too. And you will notice that the whole area is virtually litter free: please help to keep it that way.

Settle into a comfortable pace and don't be rushed. Stay alert to any potential dangers but take time to soak up the views, the abundance of flowers, the sounds and scents of the journey. Make your tour in the Vanoise an experience you will recall with pleasure years later. And unless the weather is threatening or you're running short of time, allow yourself a few minutes

PASTOU – THE SHEPHERD'S GUARD DOG

Numerous sheep graze the Vanoise pastures and in recent years the tradition of using dogs to guard the animals against attack by wolf, bear and lynx has been revived. It's quite possible that you will see one or more large white Pyrenean mountain dogs in the vicinity of a flock of sheep. Having been born and raised in the sheepfold, these *pastous* will have developed a strong bond with the animals they've been trained to look after, and will be alert to any perceived danger.

Keep your distance!

If you come across a flock of sheep, do not approach them but make a detour around the grazing area to avoid raising the attention of the *pastou*. Should one of the dogs approach, it will probably simply sniff you and, once satisfied that you present no threat, go back to the flock. Don't attempt to fuss the dog, but act passively and turn slowly away.

every hour or so to perch upon a rock and contemplate the peace and natural beauty that are among the gifts of these mountains.

RECOMMENDED MAPS

The Carte de Randonnée 1:50,000 hiking map *A3 Vanoise*, published by Rando Éditions, should be more than adequate for the treks described. The cartography by the IGN (the French national mapping agency) is excellent, as is the artistic representation of glacier, ridge and woodland. Major walking routes such as the GR5 and GR55 are boldly outlined in red, while national park boundaries are delineated in green. Refuges, *gîtes*

The welcoming refuge at L'Orgère (ToV, Stage 1)

and official campsites are also clearly marked. The map has 2km grid-squares and is GPS compatible, and a number of useful telephone numbers are given below the key. In recent years the Parc National de la Vanoise (PNV) published a very useful map at 1:60,000 but this is no longer available. If it becomes available again it is a very useful scale.

For greater detail, the IGN 1:25,000 series is excellent. For the treks described in this guide, you will need the following sheets: 3534OT and 3633ET.

EQUIPMENT

The choice of clothing and equipment for any Alpine trek can be crucial to your comfort and enjoyment. Weight is an important factor; carry

too much and each uphill will seem longer and steeper than it really is and you'll quickly tire. So think carefully and pare your load down to the very minimum. With plenty of versatile, durable lightweight equipment available, there's little point in using a heavier alternative. Through careful selection of essential items, you ought to be able to keep your

KIT LIST

- The right footwear is of prime importance. Lightweight boots that have proved to be comfortable for hillwalking should be fine.
- Socks: make sure they meet your needs and change them daily to avoid discomfort.
- Waterproofs are essential, not only for protection from rain but also to use as windproofs. A lightweight jacket and overtrousers made from a breathable fabric are recommended, as is a small collapsible umbrella (useful for those who wear glasses).
- A fleece or pile jacket is essential, for wintry conditions may be experienced above 2000m even in midsummer.
- To protect against the extremes of sunshine and heat, take a brimmed hat, high-factor sun cream, lip salve and sunglasses. Wear lightweight layers that can be removed with ease in hot weather.
- Carry a compact first-aid kit, water bottle (1 litre minimum capacity), map, guidebook, whistle, compass and a small headtorch, as well as a penknife and emergency food.
- Take a lightweight towel and basic personal toiletries (plus toilet paper and a lighter), and a sleeping bag liner for use in *gîtes* and refuges.
- Trekking poles: these have numerous uses, such as giving aid when crossing streams, helping maintain balance over rough ground and easing the strain on legs during the many steep descents.
- Your rucksack should fit comfortably, with the waist-belt adjusted to take the weight and eliminate unnecessary movement when walking. A waterproof cover is highly recommended, and you should take a large polythene bag (bin liner) for wet days. Pack your gear into stuff sacks or dry bags. Plastic bags of assorted sizes will also be useful.
- Non-essential items you might consider taking include a camera, binoculars for watching wildlife, and a notebook in which to record your experiences. A GPS could be useful, and a mobile phone for emergencies – but note that in many areas it may not be possible to get a signal, and recharging facilities are not always available.

rucksack weight down to a maximum of 8–10kg.

Unless you plan to camp, a conventional sleeping bag is unnecessary, but you will need to carry a sleeping bag liner for use in refuges and *gîtes*. One complete change of clothes should suffice. It's usually possible to wash and dry socks, T-shirts and underwear overnight.

SAFETY IN THE MOUNTAINS

The majority of the walking is on clearly marked trails, but some stages lead through lonely, wild and seemingly desolate terrain where paths are sketchy and the route is defined only by a line of cairns. There are high passes to cross and streams to negotiate, which at certain times of the year may be raging torrents that

destroy footbridges or submerge mid-season stepping stones. Be aware, too, that water levels are higher in the afternoons because of snow-melt and glacier run-off. Such uncertainties may add spice to your trek, but they can also increase the accident risk. Natural hazards abound in mountain country, and all walkers should remain alert and prepared for any emergencies that may arise.

Remember... There is no free mountain rescue service in the Alps, and an emergency can be extremely expensive for the patient and their family or friends. Be adequately insured and be cautious. The

Looking back to the Col du Grand Marchet, with two spectacular waterfalls fed by the run-off from the Glaciers de la Vanoise (TdGV, Stage 1)

SAFETY DOS AND DON'TS

- Don't attempt any of these treks too early or too late in the year.
- Ensure you are both physically and mentally prepared.
- Plan each day's stage carefully. Study the route outline, taking note of the height gain and loss and the estimated time needed to complete the stage. Note any possible shelter along the trail that could be useful in the event of a storm.
- Phone ahead to book a place at the next refuge. Phone to cancel if your plans change.
- Check the weather forecast before setting out – *gardiens* often pin a weather bulletin on the refuge noticeboard.
- Carry a few emergency rations and a first-aid kit.
- Do not overestimate your physical ability, and bear in mind the limitations of the weakest or least experienced member of your party.
- Watch for signs of deteriorating weather and turn back rather than continue into an oncoming storm or on a trail that has become dangerous.
- If your plans change and you decide not to continue to the refuge or *gîte* where you are expected, phone at the earliest opportunity to let the *gardien* know.
- Do not venture onto exposed ridges if a storm is imminent. In the event of being caught out by one, avoid isolated trees, prominent rocks or metallic objects (temporarily discard trekking poles) and refrain from taking shelter in caves, beneath overhanging rocks or in gullies. Instead, kneel or squat on your rucksack, with head down and hands on knees.
- In the unhappy event of an accident, stay calm. Move yourself and, if possible, the injured person (with care not to aggravate the injury) away from any imminent danger of stonefall or avalanche and administer first aid. Keep the victim warm, using any spare clothing available. Make a written note of the precise location where the patient can be found, and either phone for assistance using a mobile phone (if you can get a signal), or send for help while someone remains with the injured person – assuming, that is, that you're in a party of more than two people. Should there be a mountain refuge nearby, seek assistance there. If valley habitation is nearer, call 112 (the general emergency number) or contact the PGHM (mountain rescue) on 04 79 05 18 04 (Modane) or 04 79 07 01 10 (Bourg-St-Maurice). Should it be impossible to go for help, use the international mountain distress signal shown at the front of this book.

Mont Blanc dominates the northern views from the Pas de la Tovière (ToV, Stage 8)

addresses of several specialist insurance companies whose policies cover mountain walking/trekking can be found in Appendix A. It is advisable to leave a copy of your policy at home with a friend or family member and take the original with you. Reduced-cost (sometimes free) urgent medical treatment is available to EU citizens carrying a European Health Insurance Card (EHIC). From 1 January 2021 EHIC cards issued to UK citizens continue to be valid, but on expiry it is necessary to apply for a GHIC (Global Health Insurance Card). At the time of writing it's not clear how well these arrangements will work, so it is also recommended that you take out medical cover for your trip. See https://www.nhs.uk/using-the-nhs/health-care-abroad/apply-for-a-free-uk-global-health-insurance-card-ghic/.

USING THIS GUIDE

This guide contains all the information you should need to follow the two main treks described on a day-by-day basis. (Less detailed notes are provided for the shorter treks, which often share sections of the main trails.) The routes are presented in stages, each of which equates to a day's walking, but, by providing rolling times from place to place and details of accommodation where available, the guide enables you to devise an itinerary to suit your own requirements. Alternative itineraries for the main Tour of the Vanoise are suggested in the route introduction, but there's scope for more, so there's no need to stick rigidly to the schedules set out here.

Each stage is accompanied by a map showing that section of the route. These are not intended as an alternative to the topographical sheet recommended above, but rather are to be used in conjunction with it. Route profiles are also provided to illustrate the undulating nature of each trek and the facilities available along the way.

At the beginning of each stage, a route summary is given in terms of distance, the approximate amount of time needed to reach that day's destination, the high point or points to be gained, and the accumulated height gain and loss for that specific stage.

Refuge du Fond des Fours has spectacular views to the north (ToV, Stage 7 variant)

It should be noted that distances are estimates only. Where accommodation lies off the main trail, the extra distance off route is shown as +hr and +min.

Since progress on a trek is usually measured not so much by distance as by the amount of time it takes to walk from A to B, it is important to remember that times quoted are approximations only and make no allowance for rest stops, picnics, photography breaks or time taken to consult the map or guidebook. For these, you should add an extra 25–50 per cent to the day's total. Inevitably, the times given here will be considered fast by some readers and slow by others, but please remember that they are offered merely as a guide, not as a challenge. Trekking in the Vanoise is best enjoyed at a leisurely pace.

Abbreviations have been used sparingly. While most should be easily understood, the following list is provided for clarification:

- ATM: automated teller machine, cash dispenser
- BMC: British Mountaineering Council
- CAF: Club Alpin Français (now Fédération Française des Clubs Alpins et de Montagne, FFCAM)
- EHIC: European Health Insurance Card
- FFCAM: Fédération Française des Clubs Alpins et de Montagne (formerly Club Alpin Français, CAF)
- GR: Grande Randonnée, eg GR5 (a long-distance path)
- IGN: Institut National de l'Information Géographique et Forestière (the French national mapping agency)

INFORMATION AT A GLANCE

Camping: Official campsites are located in Bessans, Val d'Isère, Modane and Pralognan-la-Vanoise. Camping and bivouacking are forbidden in the national park, but an overnight pitch for small tents is allowed, for a small fee, in the vicinity of the following refuges: Arpont, Barmettes, Col du Palet, Dent Parrachée, La Femma, Fond d'Aussois, Fournache, La Leisse, Le Montana, Plan Sec, La Valette and Vallonbrun.

Currency: France uses the euro, abbreviated to €. While most credit cards are accepted in hotels and some *gîtes*, cash will be needed to pay for services in most mountain refuges. Take plenty of ready cash with you, for there are very few opportunities to withdraw from banks along the route. ATMs can be found in Modane, Val d'Isère and Pralognan-la-Vanoise.

Formalities: UK visitors will need a passport to enter France. Together with visitors from Australia, Canada and the USA (among others), UK visitors will need a visa if they intend to remain in the country for more than three months.

Health considerations: No essential inoculations are required. Avoid exposure to too much sun. Top up drinking water from approved sources. Trekkers from EU countries should carry the European Health Insurance Card (EHIC) to claim emergency medical treatment through local health services; from 1 January 2021, UK visitors can continue to use EHIC cards but on expiry must take out a new GHIC card. Medical insurance cover is essential, even where reciprocal health agreements exist (see Appendix A for a list of specialist insurers).

International dialling codes: When calling France from another country, use the international access code for that country (from the UK, the code is 00) followed by the country code for France (33), after which the initial 0 of the area code is omitted. To call the UK from France, the code is 0044.

Language: French is used everywhere within the Vanoise region but English is understood in a few refuges and hotels, although not all. Elementary French will usually suffice for most basic needs, but for anything more advanced it would be worth brushing up on your language skills before leaving home. A French–English glossary is included as Appendix C.

Mobile phones: Due to the very nature of the terrain, it is not always possible to get a signal for your mobile phone, and the possibility of recharging batteries will depend on your choice of overnight accommodation.

Mountain refuges: Always telephone ahead (or ask the hut *gardien* to do so on your behalf) to book a place in the next refuge or *gîte*, and call again if your plans change. Telephone numbers are given in the route descriptions. Remember to carry a sleeping bag liner to use in the dormitories.

Tourist information: French Tourist Office www.france.fr/fr; Parc National de la Vanoise www.vanoise-parcnational.fr/fr

Weather forecast: https://meteofrance.com or tel 3250.

- PGHM: Peloton de Gendarmerie de Haute Montagne (the mountain rescue section of the *gendarmerie*)
- PNV: Parc National de la Vanoise
- PO: post office
- TdGV: Tour des Glaciers de la Vanoise
- TGV: Train à Grande Vitesse (the superfast French train)
- ToV: Tour of the Vanoise

Routes described in this guide reflect as accurately as possible the various tours, as experienced during research. However, the mountain environment is not a static one, and changes can and do occur, resulting in paths being rerouted and certain landmarks altered. Any corrections required in order to keep the book up to date will be made in future reprints, where possible, and in the meantime will be posted on the Cicerone website (www.cicerone.co.uk/863/updates).

Should you discover any changes or be able to recommend additions with regard to accommodation, we would very much appreciate a brief note to that effect. Such information, sent via the contact form on our website (www.cicerone.co.uk/contact), will be gratefully received.

GPX tracks

GPX tracks for the routes in this guidebook are available to download free at www.cicerone.co.uk/863/GPX. A GPS device is an excellent aid to navigation, but you should also carry a map and compass and know how to use them.

COVID RESTRICTIONS

This guide was completed in summer 2021. Please check detailed regulations before traveling; the one certainty is that things will change.

Refuges may restrict numbers and enforce strict hygiene rules that must be adhered to in these confined environments. Under current French regulations (Autumn 2021), a pass demonstrating vaccination status is required to enter indoor public spaces.

In addition, your home country may impose re-entry requirements.

TOUR OF THE VANOISE

The reflective lake at Plan du Lac (Stage 5)

TREK 1
Tour of the Vanoise

Start/Finish	Modane
Distance	163km
Time	11 days
High point	Col de Chavière (2796m); Col des Fours, described as a variant, is at 2976m
Access	By train or bus to Modane via Chambéry

The valley of the Arc, known as the Maurienne, effectively separates the Vanoise massif from the Franco-Italian frontier range and receives most of the run-off from the Glaciers de la Vanoise. In its upper reaches, it is a particularly beautiful valley of open meadows, patches of larchwood and, in Le Villaron and Bonneval, two unspoilt and extremely attractive villages. The first five stages of the tour, however, explore the high country above it, only descending to the valley on the sixth day. And it is this exploration, this delving into the combes and tributary valleys that scour the high mountains, that makes such an exciting introduction to the region.

The Tour of the Vanoise (ToV) is described here in 11 stages, but there are other options, for it would be possible to complete the tour in 10 days or to extend it by visiting outlying or neighbouring valleys. Since some stages offer several overnight possibilities, a variety of itineraries could be devised to suit the ambition and inclination of each trekker and the time available. Sample itineraries are given below. Please note that times quoted for each stage do not include rest stops or photographic delays, for which you should add another 25–50 per cent.

A 10-day tour
- Stage 1 Modane to Refuge de l'Orgère (3hr)
- Stage 2 Refuge de l'Orgère to Refuge de Plan Sec via Col du Barbier (5hr)
- Stage 3 Refuge de Plan Sec to Refuge de l'Arpont (5hr 30min)
- Stage 4 Refuge de l'Arpont to Refuge du Plan du Lac (4hr 30min)
- Stage 5 Refuge du Plan du Lac to Refuge du Vallonbrun (6hr 30min)
- Stage 6 Refuge du Vallonbrun to Bonneval-sur-Arc (4hr 30min)
- Stage 7 Bonneval-sur-Arc to Val d'Isère via Col de l'Iseran (5hr 30min)

- Stage 8 Val d'Isère to Refuge de la Leisse via Col de la Leisse (7hr)
- Stage 9 Refuge de la Leisse to Chalet-Refuge Le Repoju via Col de la Vanoise (8hr)
- Stage 10 Chalet-Refuge Le Repoju to Modane via Col de Chavière (8hr 30min)

A 12-day tour
- Stages 1–8 as above
- Stage 9 Refuge de la Leisse to Refuge Entre Deux Eaux (1hr 50min), then walk to Refuge de la Femma and back to Refuge Entre Deux Eaux (6hr total)
- Stage 10 Refuge Entre Deux Eaux to Pralognan-la-Vanoise via Col de la Vanoise (5hr)
- Stage 11 Pralognan-la-Vanoise to Refuge de Péclet-Polset (5hr)
- Stage 12 Refuge de Péclet-Polset to Modane via Col de Chavière (5hr 30min)

Alternative routes via Refuge de la Femma
The main routes are described taking in Val d'Isère and Tignes. For those wanting to avoid the ski industry here, take the direct route in Stage 7A, or Stage 8A from Val d'Isère, in each case crossing the Col de la Rocheure to Refuge de la Femma. From here, follow Stage 9A to the Col de la Vanoise and Pralognan, or add another day by visiting the Refuge de la Leisse. All these routes explore a region of wild and remote landscapes. Stage 7A would fit into the schedule of a 10-day trek.

Refuge du Plan du Lac at the end of Stage 4

The Aiguille Doran dominates the skyline from the Refuge de l'Orgère (Stage 1)

The Tour of the Vanoise

On Stage 1, the route leaves workaday Modane and almost immediately strikes up the hillside on a steepening woodland trail. On a hot day it can be a gruel-ling start, with an unrelenting 900m climb to reach Refuge de l'Orgère, the first hut of the tour. This is a well-appointed refuge, located in the mouth of a combe overlooking flower meadows, with the graceful Aiguille Doran soaring behind it. Across the valley to the south and east stretches a long line of mountains, not rag-ged or dramatic, but friendly and welcoming – the perfect backdrop to the start of a long walk.

On the second day, those mountains across the Maurienne are in view as far as Col du Barbier, after which the GR5 swings north into a tributary valley con-taining two lakes overlooked by the lofty Dent Parrachée. Although considerably longer and more scenically rewarding than the first stage, this is a less demanding day which ends at one of several refuges built on the east side of the tributary. Stages 1 and 2 could be combined but would result in a long day if you're not already mountain-fit.

Stages 3 and 4 make a long loop above and around the gorge of the Doron de Termignon, which cuts into the mountains north of the village after which it is named. Gaining majestic views of the Grande Casse and Grande Motte, the route is enhanced by a series of waterfalls, streams and lakes that give mirror-like reflections of snow- and ice-draped peaks. *Bouquetin* (ibex), chamois and marmot all inhabit this fine valley, adding something special to the trekking experience.

38

Leaving Refuge du Plan du Lac, Stage 5 of the tour heads south and southeast above a few isolated alp farms, before crossing the Crête de la Turra and turning once more above the Maurienne. Descending at first through forest, then meadows full of flowers in early summer, the trail then climbs to the unmanned Refuge du Cuchet and makes a long contour across precipitous slopes hundreds of metres above the Arc river on the way to Refuge du Vallonbrun. Next day takes the route steeply down into the Haute-Maurienne, temporarily turning away from the high mountains, but exploiting the route's varied nature by visiting hamlets and villages and wandering through more Alpine meadows on the way to medieval Bonneval-sur-Arc at the southeastern limit of this Tour of the Vanoise.

Having arrived at Bonneval, roughly half the circuit has been achieved. The second half will be different and more demanding, for it visits two contrasting resorts (Val d'Isère and Pralognan-la-Vanoise), dodges in and out of the national park, and crosses several high passes. Some of the finest and most dramatic landscapes of the whole region are explored, but there are some eyesores too, courtesy of the downhill ski industry. Happily, these are soon dispensed with, and it will be the wild nature of the route that provides the greatest impact.

From Bonneval, the options open up, depending on time available, weather, conditions in the mountains, and how much you wish to avoid the ski area around Tignes:

- The main route crosses the Col de l'Iseran and descends to Val d'Isère, and the following day passes Tignes before crossing the Col de la Leisse on the GR5 (see Stages 7 and 8). This two-day routing does tangle with the ski industry of the northern Vanoise, but does not mar the route. It is the recommended option in poor weather or limited visibility.
- For those looking for a more adventurous and shorter routing, stay with the main ToV to Pont de la Neige below the Iseran, turn west to climb the Col des Fours and traverse wild mountain country on the way to the Refuge de la Femma. (This is described in Stage 7A.) The next day, rejoin the main route at Entre Deux Eaux. (This route is also taken by the Tour of the Eastern Vanoise.)
- The Col de la Rocheure and Refuge de la Femma can also be accessed directly from Val d'Isère (Stage 8A).
- An alternative to the main route after Val d'Isère is to climb the Tovière and Fresse mountains high above Tignes before rejoining the main route below the Col de la Leisse (see Stage 8). This higher route cannot avoid the ski industry entirely but has spectacular views. It is not recommended in poor conditions, and the ridge would feel more exposed in strong winds.

Leaving Bonneval, Stage 7 of the main route climbs steeply out of the valley, heading roughly northward to the Col de l'Iseran. Although this is a road pass, the ToV is barely disturbed by traffic, for the trail passes into the glorious Vallon de la Lenta and climbs through its upper gorge, hardly aware of the road's existence some way above. The north side of the Iseran is ski country, but after descending an initial scarred slope, the GR5 trail (which was rejoined in the Vallon de la Lenta) makes every effort to avoid ski tows and pistes, and snakes down to Val d'Isère through luxuriant forest.

On the eighth stage, from Val d'Isère to Refuge de la Leisse, the national park is re-entered on the approach to Col de la Leisse; this is a lovely stretch, with La Grande Motte appearing as a massive ice-topped wall above the col and the valley which lies below it. That wall extends to its loftier neighbour, La Grande Casse, and on the ninth day of the tour you wander alongside it all the way to the Col de la Vanoise. You then descend beside monstrous moraines and below the towering Aiguille de la Vanoise to reach the Lac des Vaches. This is an idyllic and picturesque site, the shallow lake being crossed on a stone causeway, below which hillsides are bathed in scarlet alpenrose. The trail plunges down these hillsides, then through forest to Pralognan-la-Vanoise, nestling in an attractive valley.

Refuge de Péclet-Polset lies near the head of that valley under the twin aiguilles from which it takes its name, and a half day's walk leads to it. Views from the refuge are very fine, with the Pointe de l'Échelle being the main focus of attention. Its west ridge dips to the rocky Col de Chavière, whose crossing is the highlight of the final day of the tour. From the col, a vast array of peaks are on show, including Mont Blanc to the north, and the rugged Écrins massif to the south.

The route then swoops down the steep south side of the col, and continues down, down and down a knee-punishing descent of nearly 1800 metres before reaching Modane, where the trek began 11 days earlier.

Looking down on the attractive Plan d'Aval lake (Stage 2); Stage 3 crosses the grassy ridge above the lake

Start	Modane (1050m)
Finish	Refuge de l'Orgère (1935m)
Distance	6km
Ascent	890m
Descent	Negligible
Time	3hr
High point	Refuge de l'Orgère (1935m)
Facilities	Modane – hotels, camping; Refuge de l'Orgère (3hr) – PNV refuge

This initial stage may be a short one, but it will be quite enough for most trekkers who have just completed a day's travel and need to settle into the rhythm of a mountain walk, for the forest trail which climbs out of the valley to Orgère can seem unrelentingly steep. However, it's a very pleasant stage, with light, spacious forest giving shade on a hot summer's day, and occasional open meadows bright with flowers. For much of the ascent, views are of Modane in the valley below, and of the Charmaix combe cutting into the Mont Thabor massif opposite.

If you start early, this stage can be combined with Stage 2, although if you are not fully fit, this would make a long first day.

Modane (1050m) is a small industrial town in two parts: Modane *gare*, which clusters around the railway station in the Fourneaux district, and Modane *ville* (the town), a few minutes' walk upvalley. Situated close to the Italian border, with both road and rail tunnels passing through the south-flanking mountains en route to Turin, the town is of strategic importance, hence the protection given by the historic Fort du Sapey built on the hillside to the northwest. Conveniently reached by rail from Chambéry, it has most services but a limited number of shops, bars and restaurants. There's a post office, several banks with ATMs, and a large supermarket on the main road on the outskirts of Modane *ville*, while the tourist office is situated on Place Sommeiller (tel 04 79 05 26 67).

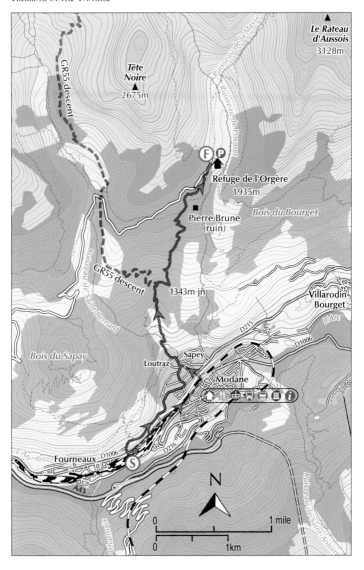

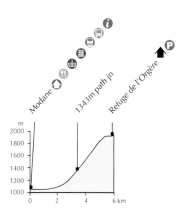

Most of the town's hotels are located opposite the station: **Hôtel de la Gare** (tel 04 79 83 26 19); **Hôtel Les Voyageurs** (tel 04 79 05 01 39); **Hôtel Le Perce-Neige** (tel 04 79 05 00 50); **Hôtel Le Commerce** (tel 04 79 05 20 98). There's also a campsite, **Camping La Vanoise** (tel 04 79 05 21 39). From the bus station (*gare routière*) next to the railway station, buses travel upvalley as far as Bonneval-sur-Arc.

There are two options to begin the walk. If you need to buy supplies for the next six days, it would be preferable to take the alternative route described below. The main route begins opposite the bus station, left of the railway station, where a sign to Refuge de l'Orgère directs the way through a small square and across the Arc river. Follow the road as it curves right, passes a few buildings, then becomes a track. About 500 metres later, join a tarmac road by the Pont Émile Charvoz. This leads through the 'suburb' of **Loutraz** and eventually brings you to a minor crossroads by a small chapel, where you meet the alternative route and turn left.

Alternative start

On leaving the railway station, bear right and wander along the main road heading upvalley. Pass a road bridge over the Arc river and continue ahead on the south side of the river. Before long, come to a Casino supermarket which gives the last opportunity to stock up with food supplies (apart from refuge packed lunches) before reaching Bessans in six days' time. Shortly after passing the supermarket, turn left on a narrow road (sign to Aussois and Le Bourget) which goes beneath the railway, then over the river to enter **Loutraz**. At a staggered crossroads go ahead, rising uphill between houses along Rue de Chavières. This brings you to another minor crossroads by a small chapel with a water supply next to it. Here, you join the main route and turn right.

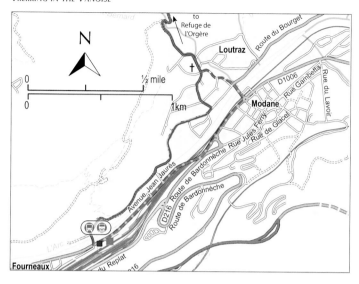

Twisting uphill, the tarmac ends by the last house, where a track continues into woodland. When the track forks, bear right across a bridge. Eventually the way

The Arc river runs alongside the railway to Italy, with the first and second stages of the tour rising high above

narrows to a footpath at a four-way crossing. Cross directly ahead, climbing steeply.

Throughout the ensuing forest section, which leads almost all the way to Orgère, there are numerous trail junctions. Each one is either signed or the route is otherwise obvious. The path is clear, well-made, narrow in places and unremittingly steep, but the forest is a delight when the fragrance of pine is drawn out by the sun's warmth. On reaching the **GR55 and GR5 path junction at 1343m** (**1hr 30min**), keep right on the GR5.

When the trail emerges from forest into a lovely open meadow near the solitary stone chalet of **Pierre Brune** (**2hr 30min**), you gain impressive views eastward through the Maurienne. Across the meadow, come onto a track. Turn right for a few paces, then left at a continuing path where a sign shows 15min to Refuge de l'Orgère.

The path re-enters forest, but contours round the hillside for 5min, then forks. Branch left and you'll soon come onto a minor road. Bear right, and a few paces later arrive at the **Refuge de l'Orgère** (**3hr**).

Refuge de l'Orgère (1935m, tel 06 51 91 83 71): Owned by the PNV, this large and comfortable refuge has excellent facilities. Overlooking flower meadows on the edge of the national park at the entrance to the Orgère combe, it enjoys fine views across the Maurienne, but being accessible by vehicle it is invariably very busy during July and August. The refuge has 70 dormitory places, full meals service and self-catering facilities. During the summer months, videos devoted to the wildlife of the region are often shown as part of the national park's education programme.

AIGUILLE DORAN AND ORGÈRE VALLEY

The sharp-pointed, pear-shaped Aiguille Doran (3041m) dominates the little valley north of the refuge. A nature trail (*sentier natur*) traverses the east flank of the valley, then curves at its head to join a track leading back to the hut, thus providing a pleasant circular walk. A high trail climbing directly above the refuge heads for Col de Chavière and Pralognan-la-Vanoise (see Stage 11 for a description of this in the reverse direction), while another cuts along the eastern side of Aiguille Doran to cross the Col de la Masse (2922m) for a challenging route to Plan Sec. The main GR5 route to Plan Sec on Stage 2 is not as demanding as this crossing but is nonetheless a visually rewarding one. The little Orgère valley is rich in wild flowers in the early summer; near its head, chamois, marmots and *bouquetin* can often be seen.

STAGE 2
Refuge de l'Orgère to Refuge de Plan Sec

Start	Refuge de l'Orgère (1935m)
Finish	Refuge de Plan Sec (2316m)
Distance	13km
Ascent	870m
Descent	490m
Time	5hr
High point	Path junction (2426m) above Plan d'Amont
Facilities	Refuge du Fond d'Aussois (4hr + 30min) – FFCAM refuge + camping; Refuge de la Dent Parrachée (4hr + 30min) – FFCAM refuge + camping; Refuge de la Fournache (4hr 15min) – refuge + camping; Refuge de Plan Sec (5hr) – privately owned refuge + camping; Chalet-Hôtel Le Montana (5hr + 10min) – privately owned refuge + camping

This full-day's stage offers plenty of scenic variety and serves as an excellent introduction to the area, as the walk to Plan Sec gradually unfolds the topography of this southern edge of the Vanoise region and provides a real flavour of what is to come in the days ahead. The route traces the national park's boundary on the GR5, for much of the way along a balcony cutting across slopes high above the Maurienne. It goes through forest and over steeply sloping pastures, soaks in a panorama of big mountains walling the south and east sides of the valley, and then makes a loop round a large combe containing a pair of small dammed lakes.

There are no major difficulties, and the ascents are much shorter and less severe than on yesterday's route. Follow the GR5 waymarking.

Descend directly below Refuge de l'Orgère on a narrow path cutting through meadows. Crossing a stream, come onto a track below a stone-built chalet and bear right. Easy walking along this track soon brings you to the group of buildings of L'Orgère (**10min**), where there's a trail junction. Turn left, now entering the **Bois du Bourget** forest.

The trail enters the national park after Col du Barbier

In its early stages, the forest trail follows a regular contour. Then it rises a little before dropping to a junction where you bear left. The way now begins to climb, crossing a series of rock and boulder tips and a minor stream; leaving the trees, it comes to a high point of 2225m. Now the path eases across high sloping pastures, rising slightly now and then, with fine views across and along the Maurienne where sentry-like peaks guard the valley.

Contouring 1000m above the valley bed, the trail brings you to a pair of stone huts, marked as **Le Barbier** on the map. About 5min beyond the second of these huts, note a water supply on the left of the trail below a chalet. The way now descends to the broad grassy saddle of **Col du Barbier** (2295m, **2hr**), from which the village of Aussois can be seen down in the valley.

The trail maintains its descent as far as a signed junction. Ignore the right branch, which drops steeply to the dam at the southern end of the Plan d'Aval lake and then continues to the village of Aussois in the Maurienne. Instead, take the left-hand trail heading northward along the west flank of the deep combe of the Aussois valley, on the far side of which La Dent Parrachée (3697m) is the main feature, soaring above two lakes. A broad track may be seen carving a way across the lower slopes of this mountain, with a group of three tiny-looking buildings just above it. These buildings together comprise the Refuge de Plan Sec.

Climbing to a high point of 2391m, the way then enters a broad, open area littered with rocks and running with streams. Heading roughly north-west, the trail slopes gently downhill. Another path cuts off to the right. Ours

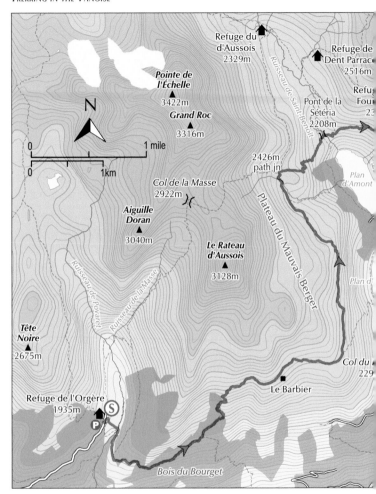

continues into a gully to the left of a large rock-and-grass-covered bluff, then rises alongside a stream to meet another **path junction at 2426m (3hr 30min)**. The left branch here climbs to Col de la Masse above Refuge de l'Orgère, but we bear right, crossing a stream to pass round the northern side of the bluff

before descending steeply to a saddle of grass and alpenroses overlooking Plan d'Amont – a fine vantage point. From here, the trail continues its descent as far as a bridge spanning the torrent of Ruisseau de Saint-Benoît. This bridge is known as the **Pont de la Sétéria** (2208m) and is reached after a 20min descent from the 2426m path junction. A sign here suggests 1hr to Plan Sec.

PLAN D'AVAL AND PLAN D'AMONT

In early summer, this section of the route along the west flank of the Aussois valley is not only vibrant with crimson alpenrose but adorned with flowers almost everywhere. The terrain is rugged but immensely attractive (stay alert for the possible sighting of chamois and marmot), with rocks, boulders and streams on the hillsides, enticing views of the walling rim of mountains, and the two lakes below. The most southerly of these lakes (Plan d'Aval) is noted for the pipe spewing a jet of water which has been diverted for 17km through the mountains from the head of the Doron gorge, in order to serve the hydro station at Avrieux. The upper lake (Plan d'Amont) is a deep green in colour and is the more attractive of the two.

There are no fewer than five refuges in the Aussois valley, although not all are conveniently placed to be of use here. The first (Refuge du Fond d'Aussois) may be reached by a 30min signed diversion from the Pont de la Sétéria.

Refuge du Fond d'Aussois (2329m, tel 04 79 20 39 83): This FFCAM-owned refuge has 52 dormitory places, plus camping space. A 20-place winter room is permanently open.

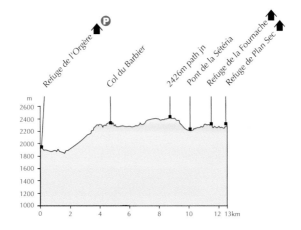

At the head of the valley, the **Col d'Aussois** (2914m) provides a crossing for walkers tackling the shorter Tour des Glaciers de la Vanoise on a stage coming from Pralognan-la-Vanoise.

Cross the bridge and climb the slope ahead, taking care if late winter snow still covers the trail on the initial steeply sloping section, and about 20min or so from the bridge you come to two more marked junctions in close succession.

Looking across the deep valley to the Dent Parrachée

These offer the chance to visit either **Refuge de la Fournache** (5min) or Refuge de la Dent Parrachée (in 30min).

Refuge de la Fournache (2390m, tel 06 09 38 72 38): Overlooking the main trail, the refuge has 34 dormitory places and offers the possibility of camping nearby.

Refuge de la Dent Parrachée (2516m, tel 04 79 20 32 87): This refuge is 30min off the route. It is FFCAM-owned, with 42 dormitory places plus camping space, and the 30-place winter room is permanently open.

Below the second of these junctions, the path cuts down across pastures and over two streams draining the Vallon de la Fournache. A few paces beyond the second of these, bear left up a path which rises directly to a dirt road/track. Turn right along this for about 15min, then take a narrow path slanting up the left-hand slope to gain the three buildings of the **Refuge de Plan Sec** (**5hr**).

Refuge de Plan Sec (2316m, tel 04 79 20 31 31): This attractive, privately owned refuge has been converted from a summer farm. With 52 dormitory places, it also has limited camping space and a full meals service. Of the three buildings, one contains sleeping accommodation, another (the former stable) houses the dining room, while in the third will be found the showers and toilets.

Chalet-Hôtel Le Montana (2190m, tel 04 79 20 31 47): If all accommodation is taken at Plan Sec, try Le Montana, a further 10–15min along the track. It has 60 places, camping space and meals provision, and is open from early July to mid August.

The Plan Sec refuge is a welcoming and attractive overnight stop

STAGE 3
Refuge de Plan Sec to Refuge de l'Arpont

Start	Refuge de Plan Sec (2316m)
Finish	Refuge de l'Arpont (2309m)
Distance	16km
Ascent	750m
Descent	760m
Time	5hr 30min
High point	Above La Turra (2462m)
Facilities	Chalet-Hôtel Le Montana (+ 10min) – privately owned refuge + camping; Refuge de l'Arpont (5hr 30min) – PNV refuge + camping

On the way from Plan Sec to Arpont, you begin to experience the true nature of this remarkable region. Rounding the southern spur of Pointe de Bellecôte, the trail gains a hint of a wilder and more robust country, a contrast of high crags dashed with snow and ice, and low-lying pastures with forest at mid height. Then, crossing more projecting spurs, the Doron gorge is suddenly observed slicing through mountains that grow in stature towards the north, and which will be seen in all their glory on Stage 4.

As you draw closer to Refuge de l'Arpont, the hanging glaciers of Belle Place, Mahure and Arpont spill cascades over wayside cliffs. The final approach crosses one stream after another, their mini ravines having been carved into the plateau leading to the refuge. *Bouquetin* frequent the meadows and rocky places near the refuge, while marmots may be seen almost anywhere on this stage of the walk.

From Plan Sec, descend to the track and bear left along it. Just before reaching ski tows, the track forks. Take the lower option, which continues straight ahead, and when it makes a right-hand hairpin soon after, take a signed footpath going off to the left; this cuts through pastures, with views to the south side of the Maurienne valley.

Chalet-Hôtel Le Montana (2150m, tel 04 79 20 31 47): To visit Le Montana, instead of taking the signed footpath to the left, continue ahead for a further 10–15min. See Stage 2 for details.

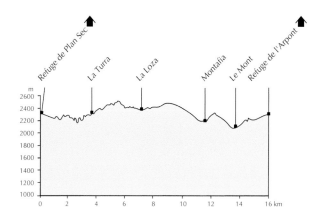

The route now makes a steady traverse on grass slopes high above the valley, working roughly northeast. The slope steepens, though the trail contours, and eventually brings you to the base of a gully into which you turn at a fork. The path climbs with zigzags through this gully as far as a junction. At this point, one route continues to climb to Grasse Combe, but ours swings to the right and edges against overhanging cliffs before coming to a spectacular section where the trail has been cut into a precipitous slope. Contouring across, you then twist up a spur in easy windings to gain a broad grass saddle and another trail junction. This is **La Turra** (2363m, **1hr 15min**). (A trail descends from here to the village of Sardières by way of the Monolithe de Sardières, a 93m tooth of rock jutting from the forest.)

From La Turra, take the path to the left. This climbs in easy zigzags up the slopes of the Roc des Corneilles to reach the day's high point of 2462m. It then

Trekkers on La Turra

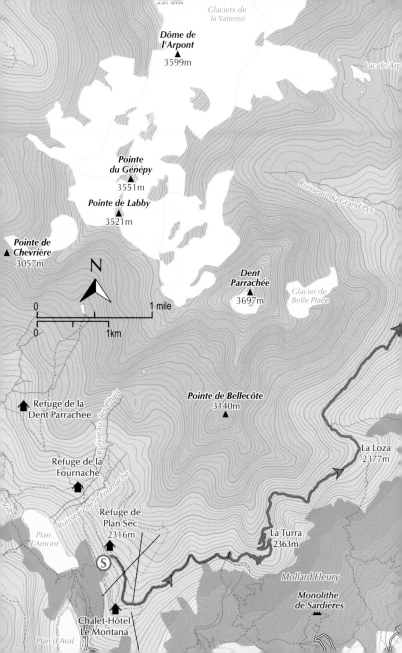

Glaciers de
la Vanoise

**Dôme de
l'Arpont**
3599m

Lac de l'Arp

**Pointe
du Génépy**
3551m

Ruisseau du Grand Pyx

Pointe de Labby
3521m

▲ **Pointe de
Chevrière**
3057m

**Dent
Parrachée**
3697m

Glacier de
Belle Place

N

0   1 mile

0   1km

Pointe de Bellecôte
3140m ▲

Ruisseau des Chaix

▲ Refuge de la
Dent Parrachée

La Loza
2377m

Refuge de la
Fournache

Ruisseau de la Fournache

Refuge de
Plan Sec
2316m ▲

La Turra
2363m

Ⓢ

*Plan
d'Amont*

Mollard Fleury

**Monolithe
de Sardières**

Chalet-Hôtel
Le Montana ▲

Plan d'Aval

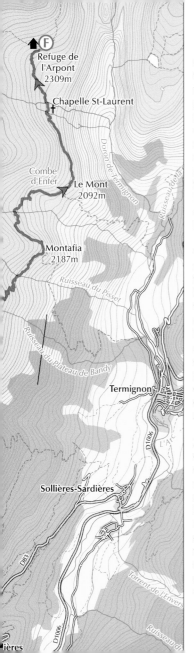

eases to the right on a long contouring traverse of a steep-walled combe, at the far side of which you reach a second grass saddle and yet another junction of paths. Ruins may be seen below the trail on the right, with a small wooden hut nearby. This area is known as **La Loza** (2377m, **2hr 30min**). If you stray for a moment to the small hill east of the junction, there are extensive views which include La Grande Casse and La Grande Motte some way to the north beyond the Doron gorge.

Follow the contouring trail as it veers slightly left from this saddle (the right-hand path offers another descent to Sardières) and cuts into a deep scoop below La Dent Parrachée, drained by the Ruisseau de Bonne Nuit. The trail is clear, though narrow in places, and early in the season may be partly covered by snowfields – in which case take extra care when crossing. At one point the trail picks its way across a rockfall. Termignon can be seen far below at the confluence of two valleys: those of the Arc (Haute-Maurienne) and the Doron.

The path climbs to a high point of 2441m, then descends to cross a smaller combe with streams running through it. Over the main stream, the trail rises once more and tops a bluff marked on the map as **Montafia** (2187m, **4hr**), where there is a ruined building at a trail junction. Ignoring the right-hand option (which descends steeply to Termignon), continue to rise, steadily at first, then more steeply in zigzags, before cutting into the shallow **Combe d'Enfer**. At its head, the Glacier de la Mahure, along with other

55

icefields below the Dômes du Génépy, forms the southern limit of the Glaciers de la Vanoise – the major ice sheet of the whole Vanoise region.

Combe d'Enfer is a delight of streams, cascades, crags, rough pastures and alpenroses. Sloping downhill on its north flank, the way passes a simple alp farm, and a few minutes later comes to a collection of ruins, **Le Mont** (2092m, **4hr 45min**). Another path descends from here to Termignon, while ours continues ahead, now high above the Doron gorge, sneaking through alder thickets. As the way progresses, so the vegetation changes and alpenroses appear in patches along the hillside. The slab face of the Pointe de la Réchasse appears to be blocking the head of the valley and entices from the north. Other big mountains crowd the horizon, and before long Refuge de l'Arpont may be seen on the hillside ahead.

The valley grows more beautiful and inspiring the deeper you wander into it. Waterfalls cascade from cliffs on the left. One footbridge after another takes the trail across streams digging channels through the rock; ruined stone huts ments can be seen on either side of the path, and the simple little **Chapelle St-Laurent** stands beside the trail; then more streams to cross, pastures starred with flowers and glacial remnants high above to the left. At last, the trail makes its final slant up and across an easy slope to reach the **Refuge de l'Arpont** (**5hr 30min**).

Alpenroses decorate the trail towards the Refuge de l'Arpont

Refuge de l'Arpont (2309m, tel 09 82 12 42 13): Renovated and enlarged in recent years, the refuge now has 94 dormitory places, plus overnight camping space. Out of season, the 24-place winter room is permanently open.

DÔME DE CHASSEFORÊT AND THE GLACIER DE L'ARPONT

The modern Refuge de l'Arpont has a magnificent outlook. Although mountains at the head of the valley cannot be seen from here (you have to walk up the trail a short distance to gain these views), the refuge commands all the valley to the south from its prominent position on the south flank of a spur jutting from the Dôme de Chasseforêt. A gleam of snow and ice forms a pelmet to the west, while the Doron gorge is a shadowed hint below to the east and southeast. *Bouquetin* can sometimes be seen grazing nearby, while marmots inhabit the neighbourhood.

West of the refuge, what's left of the Glacier de l'Arpont is plastered down the face of the Dôme de l'Arpont, a frozen cascade barely visible from the actual building. At the foot of the glacier, some 350m above the hut, lies the small Lac de l'Arpont. Given time, energy and favourable conditions, it would be worth scrambling up to this tarn to enjoy its prestigious situation and some tremendous views. Allow 2hr–2hr 30min for the round trip.

STAGE 4
Refuge de l'Arpont to Refuge du Plan du Lac

Start	Refuge de l'Arpont (2309m)
Finish	Refuge du Plan du Lac (2364m)
Distance	13.5km
Ascent	730m
Descent	680m
Time	4hr 30min
High point	Above Lacs des Lozières (2560m)
Facilities	Refuge Entre Deux Eaux (3hr 15min + 20min) – privately owned refuge; Refuge de la Femma (3hr 15min + 2hr) – PNV refuge + camping; Refuge du Plan du Lac (4hr 30min) – PNV refuge

Without question, this stage is one of the great walks of the tour; a horseshoe loop with tremendous views practically every step of the way. There's an extremely varied terrain, a good possibility of watching wildlife, a bounty of Alpine flowers, and prospects of diverting into another valley for those so inclined. The basic route is an undulating one that works its way along the western hillside heading north under the Glaciers de la Vanoise towards Mont Pelve, Pointe de la Réchasse and Pointe Mathews, the south summit of La Grande Casse. The big wall linking the Grande Casse with La Grande Motte is an impressive feature at the head of the Doron de Termignon's valley, and almost from the start it draws you towards it. A number of streams are crossed, a huge moraine bank and various post-glacial lakes are skirted, and pastures wandered before descending steeply to the confluence of the Leisse and Rocheure torrents below the lovely alp farm-turned-refuge Entre Deux Eaux. The way then curves southward across the mouth of the Vallon de la Rocheure, and climbs a grass- and shrub-covered hillside to reach the PNV-owned Refuge du Plan du Lac, with its views west to the dazzling snow and ice of the Vanoise glaciers.

Walkers tackling only the western circuit, the Tour des Glaciers de la Vanoise, will leave the main route on this stage, traversing the eastern slopes of Pointe de la Réchasse to join the route to Col de la Vanoise and Pralognan (see Tour des Glaciers de la Vanoise, Stage 4).

An alternative option would be to follow the main route as described as far as the mouth of the Vallon de la Rocheure, but instead of climbing south to Plan du Lac, continue eastward through the Rocheure valley to spend a night at Refuge de la Femma. Sufficient time would then be available next day to explore this beautiful valley before returning downstream, and then walking up to Refuge du Plan du Lac, thus adding a day to the overall tour. Other approaches to the Refuge de la Femma are described as alternative routes from Bonneval and Val d'Isère (see Stages 7A and 8A of this tour).

Heading upvalley from Arpont, the trail strikes northeastward, then rises with a few zigzags to the north, soon gaining views to a group of big mountains blocking the valley in an impressive amphitheatre. Care is required when snow remains on this section of the path, which is exposed in places. Reaching a high shelf, the route then descends a little to cross a shallow basin where easy-angled slabs are running with streams. In the early summer, some of these streams can be challenging to cross, for there are no bridges and the route is merely guided by cairns. **Caution is advised.**

Beyond these, you rise to a minor plateau – a gently sloping hillside dotted with small pools beside the trail. The trail skirts the left-hand side of the plateau, while the cliffs of Mont Pelve, Roche Ferran and Pointe de la Réchasse rise abruptly out of the landscape ahead in a formidable wall. Refuge du Plan du Lac may be seen to the east across the head of the Doron gorge.

The trail opens out, with some magnificent views towards the Glacier de la Vanoise

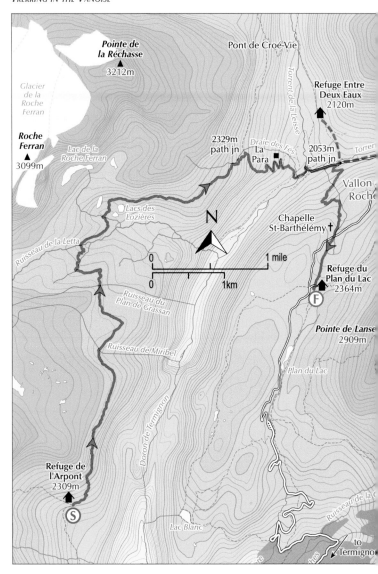

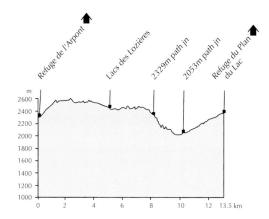

Cross a grassy bluff, then descend leftwards into a stony basin below the pointed Dôme des Sonnailles and the Glacier du Pelve which flows from it. The left-bank lateral moraine of this glacier towers on the north side of the basin.

> Above this moraine to the north, walled by the upper crags of Roche Ferran, lie the beautiful **Lac de la Roche Ferran** and the smaller **Lac du Pelve**. It is possible to reach these tarns by following up the bank of the stream which drains from them.

The glacial torrent of the **Ruisseau de la Letta** is crossed on a footbridge before the trail bears right to trace the stream's left bank, then curves to cross a second torrent – the one which comes from the tarns below Roche Ferran. You then pass between the two **Lacs des Lozières** (**2hr**), go up some glacier-polished slabs, pass above another tarn and continue to climb gently with fine views ahead. At one point it is possible to see down into the head of the Doron gorge, while the Vallon de la Rocheure (leading to the Femma refuge) stretches enticingly ahead in the east. Above the entrance to that valley, an impressive shattered crest towers over green pastures. Looking back to the southwest, the Glaciers de la Vanoise appear as a dome of ice and snow. It is along this section of trail that you reach the day's high point.

Crossing one of the streams on the trail to the Lacs des Lozières

Set among rolling grassland, not far from where the path begins to descend to the confluence of two valleys, a large 'acorn cup' stone is thought to have been carved by Neolithic man. A short way down this path, come to a signpost and a **2329m path junction** at Mont de la Para (**2hr 45min**).

The continuing path heading north is used by walkers on the Tour des Glaciers de la Vanoise. Our route bears right and continues down the slope, a steep trail twisting in numerous zigzags until it joins a farm track just below a semi-ruined stone barn near the chalets of **La Para**. The gradient eases, but you desert the track again in favour of a narrow path by a ruin and cut down through pastures to the valley bed. Follow a track round to the Doron river and wander upstream along the track to a stream confluence and a **2053m path junction** just above; the first stream is the Torrent de la Leisse, the second the Torrent de la Rocheure. The track takes you over both of these and onto a tarmac road. Wander up this road for about 300 metres, then break away to the right on a signed footpath.

At this point, there are options to visit Refuge Entre Deux Eaux (15–20min off the main route) or Refuge de la Femma in the Vallon de la Rocheure (as mentioned in the introduction to this stage and described below).

Refuge Entre Deux Eaux (2120m, tel 04 79 05 27 13): Shortly before reaching the signed footpath to the right, descend by a track sloping downhill to the left. This recrosses the Torrent de la Rocheure, then rises easily to gain the privately owned refuge in 20min. The refuge has 38 dormitory places and is open from early June until late September.

Refuge de la Femma option

Follow the road heading east for about 1.5km until it makes a sharp hairpin to the right. Now continue ahead on a track that works its way deeper into the Vallon de la Rocheure, crosses to the north bank of the river, and soon after ends at the Chalet de la Rocheure. A footpath continues over pastures and comes to Refuge de la Femma (2hr from the start of this diversion).

Refuge de la Femma (2352m, tel 04 79 05 45 40): PNV-owned, with 64 dormitory places plus camping space. There's a resident *gardien* from mid June to late September. Out of season, a winter room is permanently open, with 24 places.

The main route to Plan du Lac climbs easily among lush vegetation, passes below a cascade, and steadily gains height to reach an extensive grassland. Come onto the road again by the **Chapelle St-Barthélémy** (2284m). Cross the road and rise gently through open pastures, at the head of which there are three orientation tables. Just beyond these you come to the **Refuge du Plan du Lac** (**4hr 30min**).

Refuge du Plan du Lac (2364m, tel 04 79 20 50 85): Owned by the PNV, it has 42 dormitory places, full meals service and a resident *gardien* from June to the end of September.

PLAN DU LAC AND LA GRANDE CASSE

The Refuge du Plan du Lac is a well-appointed hut, made busy in the daytime by virtue of the road which passes nearby. No private vehicles are permitted along this road beyond Bellecombe, a parking area half an hour's walk to the south, but a summer shuttle bus service (*navette*) ferries passengers between Termignon, in the Maurienne, and the Pont de la Rocheure below Entre Deux Eaux. This shuttle bus is understandably popular with daytrippers in the high summer, as well as with walkers and climbers who use it to shortcut an otherwise long approach from the Haute-Maurienne.

The refuge enjoys a favoured location, set as it is on a flat meadow with extensive views west across the unseen Doron gorge to the Glaciers de la Vanoise, and north to La Grande Casse (3855m) and La Grande Motte (3653m). The highest summit in the Vanoise Alps, La Grande Casse received its first ascent in 1860 from William Mathews, one of the founders of the Alpine Club, and his guide Michel Croz, who was to lose his life five years later following the first ascent of the Matterhorn with Edward Whymper. The summit dome and glaciers of La Grande Motte, just visible above the wall of the Vallon de la Leisse, are laced with ski tows and cableways made accessible from Val Claret, which has resulted in an unnatural indent in the national park's boundary line.

A short walk west of the refuge provides a spectacular view into the Doron gorge, while the beautiful lake which lends its name to the Plan du Lac is reached in 10min heading downvalley. Its eastern shoreline is skirted on Stage 5.

STAGE 5
Refuge du Plan du Lac to Refuge du Vallonbrun

Start	Refuge du Plan du Lac (2364m)
Finish	Refuge du Vallonbrun (2272m)
Distance	18.5km
Ascent	720m
Descent	810m
Time	6hr 30min
High point	On the route to La Turra (c2400m); above Plan de la Cha (2366m)
Facilities	Refuge du Cuchet (4hr 30min) – PNV refuge (unmanned); Refuge du Vallonbrun (6hr 30min) – PNV refuge + camping

This is the longest stage of the tour so far, but since there are few steep uphill sections to counterbalance a rather wearisome descent from the ridge-spur of Crête de la Turra, which effectively marks the southeastern end of the Doron valley, the physical demands are not excessive.

The trail is a good one all the way from Plan du Lac to Vallonbrun. It's a scenically interesting one too, for the day begins with classic views across the Doron's gorge to the Glaciers de la Vanoise, soon adds high mountain reflections in a lake, exchanges these for a panorama that includes much of the route wandered two days ago, then includes a view south across the Haute-Maurienne to Col du Mont Cenis and Pointe de Ronce. And in early summer this stage will be one of the very finest in terms of mountain flowers; as a result, the overall time to reach Vallonbrun is likely to be far greater than the basic walking time quoted above.

Before the route loses the influence of the Doron de Termignon's valley, it curves round an immense pastoral hillside below the Crête de Côte Chaude. A few small farmsteads stand dwarfed by the enormity of this hillside and overlook the serpentine writhings of the road to Termignon, while La Dent Parrachée dominates the view west.

Once the Crête de la Turra has been turned, the trail descends steeply into forest before a track progresses the route eastward. Following the GR5, the tour now rises to the unmanned Refuge du Cuchet and continues beyond it on a belvedere of a trail high above the valley, to conclude at the charming Vallonbrun refuge.

Departing Plan du Lac, head south on an easy path across almost level pasture-land, and after about 15min come to the **lake** which, in clear conditions, provides wonderful inverted views of La Grande Casse and La Grande Motte to the north. Pass along the left-hand (eastern) side of the lake and, soon after, cut through a grassy cleft in the hills. Once you are through this cleft, the peaks on the south side of the Maurienne show as a wall ahead. About 30min from the refuge, the trail descends to **Bellecombe** (2307m), a large parking area and bus stop for the shuttle service between Termignon and the Pont de la Rocheure.

Immediately before the parking area, turn left on a track signed to Refuge du Cuchet. Winding among rolling hills, the track crosses a saddle and traverses left into a huge curving basin topped by the Crête de Côte Chaude. Pass a small farm building on the right of the track and continue as far as another farm, La Femma (**1hr 30min**), where the track ends.

BEAUFORT – THE LOCAL CHEESE

A cheese course invariably forms part of the evening meal in Vanoise refuges, and Beaufort (named for the region between the Vanoise and the Mont Blanc massif) is often chosen since it's a speciality of the region and a favourite of the locality. Beaufort has a distinctive nutty flavour, apparently derived from the rich flora of the pasturelands where the dairy cattle graze. These herds give high-quality milk which, following traditional methods when rennet is added, is transformed by the dairymen into curds. These are then cut into flakes and heated to specified temperatures before being pressed into the beechwood moulds, known as *cloches de soutirage*, that give the cheese its recognisable crust and shape. Each flat millstone-shaped cheese, weighing 30–40kg, is passed through a vat of brine and stored in damp cellars for at least six months at a constant temperature of 10°C, during which it is turned twice a week until it has matured sufficiently to be offered for sale – then cut into slices on a ref-uge table. (See www.mons-cheese.co.uk/bleu-de-termignon.)

A narrow footpath leads on, sweeping round the hillside. Rising gently, it then loses a little height and grants views north, back to the head of the valley of the Doron de Termignon, and over to the west where the trail to Arpont (taken on Stage 3) can be seen.

With a small group of farm buildings seen ahead, the path cuts across the hillside to pass above them. It eases along a rib, then goes up between the rocks of **La Turra de Termignon** (2305m, **2hr 15min**) at the end of the Crête de la Turra spur, which effectively forms the gateway to the Doron de Termignon's valley.

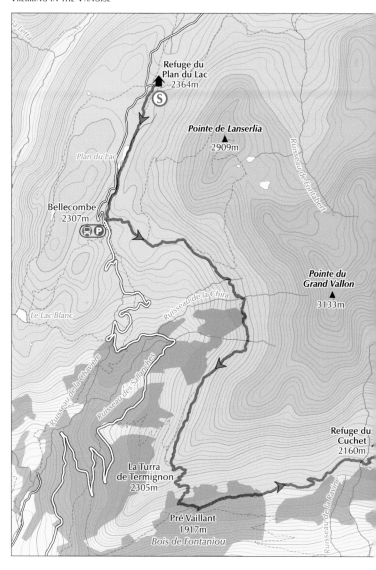

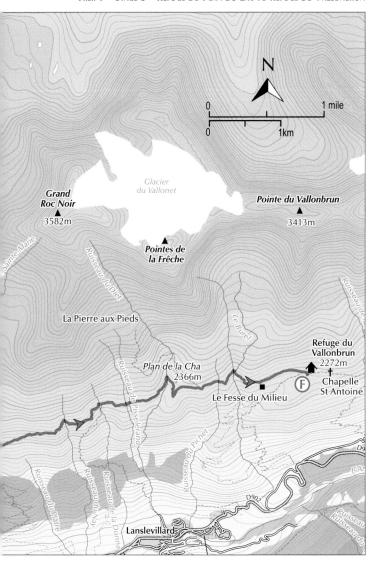

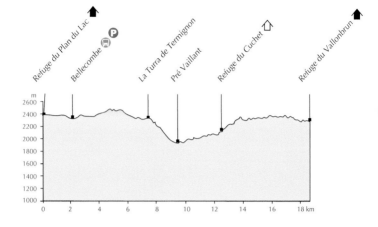

Refuge du Plan du Lac

Bellecombe

La Turra de Termignon

Pré Vaillant

Refuge du Cuchet

Refuge du Vallonbrun

This is an impressive site. Termignon is almost 1000m below; and at the edge of the crest, two contrasting valleys with different vegetation and different mountain architecture are spread before you.

The trail now descends steeply below farm buildings known as the Chalets de la Turra and goes through a natural rock garden – perhaps the most spectacular display of flowers on the whole tour. Below this, you enter forest. The way is

Crossing the wide grassy bowl before dropping down at La Turra de Termignon

The unmanned Refuge du Cuchet

unrelentingly steep and twisting, with the loss of nearly 400m of altitude. On this forest descent, the path forks, and you bear left to continue down to a crossing track marked as **Pré Vaillant** (1917m, **3hr**) where you turn left, now cutting through the Bois de Fontaniou.

Emerging from the forest by a stone barn, the track continues between open meadows, winding gently on, tracing a regular contour and with views along the Maurienne valley. Just before coming to a stone chalet, a footpath cuts left, signed to Refuge du Cuchet in 20min. Climbing across more flower-covered slopes, the trail then eases before coming to a stream. Over this, the path resumes its ascent of the hillside, steeper now on the final climb to the **Refuge du Cuchet** (**4hr 30min**).

Refuge du Cuchet (2160m, tel 04 79 62 30 54): This unmanned hut is perched high above the valley in a dramatic location on a small spur. Owned by the PNV, it has 24 dormitory places, kitchen facilities and splendid views.

Pass alongside the refuge and continue on a high route that goes up across the steeply plunging mountainside. The route then enters and crosses a brief combe, and contours out of it before descending slightly into a second combe. After this, the trail rises briefly before coming to a stream and a path junction. Here, the right fork drops to Le Coin Bas and Lanslevillard, while our route continues ahead along the GR5.

Crossing two narrow ravines, the way eases along the hillside before curving into a large combe, or hanging valley, below the Grand Roc Noir (3582m). Over a major stream which drains through this combe, go up a slope to a junction of paths at **Plan de la Cha** (2366m, **5hr 30min**). The sign here shows 45min for the final section of the walk to Vallonbrun.

The path which cuts to the left climbs to the curious **Pierre aux Pieds**, a huge block of schistose rock on which dozens of small feet were carved, possibly 7000 years ago.

Bear slightly right to climb a moraine bank, then bear left. At a crossing track, bear right then left on the continuing path. One further hillside spur is crossed, then you descend on a gentle sloping path into the lovely pastureland of Vallonbrun. Pass the few farm buildings of **La Fesse du Milieu** (note the overlapping slab roofs) and come onto a narrow road directly opposite the **Refuge du Vallonbrun** (**6hr 30min**).

Refuge du Vallonbrun (2272m, tel 04 79 05 93 93): Owned by the PNV, the refuge has 27 dormitory places in four-bed sections, camping space, full meals provision, kitchen facilities, and a resident *gardien* from June to mid September. The winter room is permanently open.

GLACIER DE L'ARCELLE NEUVE AND THE GRAND ROC NOIR

Vallonbrun is a peaceful back-country, with good views south across the deep and narrow Maurienne to the rapidly shrinking Glacier de l'Arcelle Neuve which lies across the face of Signal du Grand Mont Cenis, with Pointe de Ronce nearby. The refuge also provides good views to the west, while its eastern outlook is limited by the slope leading to a small chapel and a handful of chalets.

To the north, a long wall of mountains, topped by the Grand Roc Noir, stretches eastward before curving gently to the northeast, unbroken between the Doron de Termignon and Col de l'Iseran, and rarely dropping below 3000m. Several small glaciers lie below that ridge wall, most of which drain northward into the Vallon de la Rocheure.

STAGE 6
Refuge du Vallonbrun to Bonneval-sur-Arc

Start	Refuge du Vallonbrun (2272m)
Finish	Bonneval-sur-Arc (1810m)
Distance	16km
Ascent	180m
Descent	640m
Time	4hr 30min
High point	Chapelle St-Antoine (2300m)
Facilities	Bessans (2hr 15min) – *gîte*, hotels, camping; Le Villaron (2hr 30min) – *gîte*; Bonneval (4hr 30min) – *gîte*, hotel, chalets, FFCAM refuge

For the first time since setting out from Modane, the route now revisits the valley of the Arc (known here as the Haute-Maurienne), giving an opportunity to restock with supplies. Temporarily deserting the high country, the Tour of the Vanoise is not being disloyal – there's no alternative – but rewards the trekker with a fresh perspective. The valley walk from Col de la Madeleine to Bonneval-sur-Arc, along what is known as the Chemin du Petit Bonheur, has much to commend it, especially in early summer when the meadows are in full bloom. A short detour across the Arc gives access to Bessans; later, the trail passes through the hamlet of Le Villaron, and the stage ends in the finest of all Maurienne villages, Bonneval, whose vernacular architecture is an extremely attractive feature at the foot of the mountains.

The day begins with a walk up the dirt road for about 200 metres to reach the little **Chapelle St-Antoine** (2300m). Immediately beyond this, take a footpath signed to Collet which slopes down through pastures. At a junction of paths, bear right and soon pass a collection of ruins. The trail steepens in zigzags, descending a hillside lavish with flowers, and an hour from Vallonbrun reaches the valley floor at the Col de la Madeleine (1760m, **1hr**) and the nearby hamlet of **Le Collet**.

> **Le Collet** consists of several stone chalets and a small chapel built in 1603; a water supply is located next to the chapel. A massive landslip once blocked the valley here, and the consequent build-up of water created a huge lake on what is now the Bessans plain.

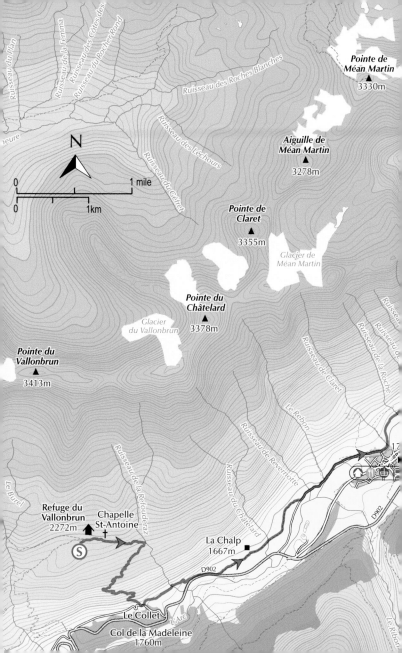

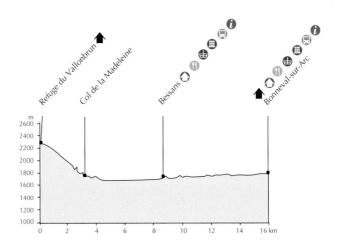

Wander along the road for a few paces, but when it begins to bear right by a ruin, take a narrow path on the left. This takes you along a little raised 'causeway' between meadows (magnificent with flowers before the grass has been cut) and with lovely views ahead. The way is obvious, and it eventually brings you onto the main valley road where you continue ahead for a short distance until it makes a right-hand curve. Leave the road for a track which cuts off left to **La Chalp** (1667m) – a few stone chalets and another simple chapel. The track eases along the valley and after about an hour from the road brings you to a bridge leading across the Arc to the village of **Bessans (2hr 15min)**.

Bessans (1710m) gives the first opportunity since Modane to restock with food supplies. It has a small selection of shops and restaurants, post office, and a tourist office just off the main square (tel 04 79 05 96 52). For accommodation, there's a 36-place *gîte d'étape*, **Le Petit Bonheur** (tel 04 79 05 06 71), and hotels: **Le Grand Fond** (tel 04 79 05 83 05) and **La Vanoise** (tel 04 79 05 96 79). There are also two campsites: **Camping de l'Illaz** (tel 06 45 89 02 32), open from June to early September; and **La Grange du Traverole** (tel 06 87 58 18 51).

WOODCARVINGS IN BESSANS

Bessans was largely destroyed in 1944 during World War II, but it has been rebuilt in traditional style. Tradition is still very much a part of the community, not only in its architecture, but in the craft of woodcarving and the wearing of local costumes during major festivals. The Maurienne region in general (and Bessans in particular) has a long tradition of woodcarving going back to the 17th century. Two hundred years later, a local craftsman, Étienne Vincendet, was the first to carve the famous *diable de Bessans* – the legendary 'devil of Bessans'.

Among the oldest buildings in the village, the Chapelle St-Antoine dates from the 14th century, but was restored 500 years later. Containing a number of 15th-century frescos illustrating the life of Christ, the chapel also has a Renaissance ceiling decorated with stars, while outside murals depict both virtues and vices. Although still used for services, the chapel is very much a museum.

In winter, Bessans has more than 80km of cross-country ski trails, and a few modest tows.

Unless you have a wish to do so, there's no need to cross into Bessans, for the route remains on the north bank of the river as a track, which you follow all the way to Le Villaron. It makes an easy, pleasant walk, with the river for company much of the way. On the opposite side of the river, the narrow Vallée d'Avérole cuts back deeply into the mountains and is dominated by Pointe de Charbonnel (3752m). It's a beautiful unspoilt valley with a small amount of habitation, and the FFCAM-owned Refuge d'Avérole tucked just below the frontier ridge.

The route along this riverside track is no longer the GR5 (which takes a high route and avoids Bonneval, although it does have a descent option), but the GR55E, also known as the Chemin du Petit Bonheur. Eventually this narrows alongside woodland, and rising gently about 35min from Bessans you come to open meadows, across which you enter the attractive stone-built hamlet of **Le Villaron** (1750m, **2hr 30min**).

> **La Bâtisse** (tel 04 79 83 14 51): Overnight accommodation in Le Villaron may be found at this *gîte d'étape*, which has 28 dormitory places and full meals provision, and is open throughout the year.

When walking through **Le Villaron**, be careful not to take the path signed to Bonneval in 4hr 30min, as this climbs above the hamlet to rejoin the GR5 – unless, of course, you have abundant energy and time. The correct path to take along the valley reaches Bonneval in less than 2hr.

Follow the road as it curves to the right to leave Le Villaron, but then take another track cutting ahead at a sharp right-hand bend by a tiny chapel dedicated

Passing under the Rocher du Château

to St Bernard. Remaining on the west bank of the Arc, the track continues between meadows and through patches of woodland, curving beneath the huge, black-streaked block of the **Rocher du Château** (1836m).

> At first glance, the **Rocher du Château** appears to block the valley midway between Bessans and Bonneval, but in fact it stands on the west side of the river where the valley narrows. (On the east bank, via ferrata routes have been created on the steep crags of Pointe d'Andagne.) The Rocher is an impressive detached block of serpentine on which eight deer were painted in Neolithic

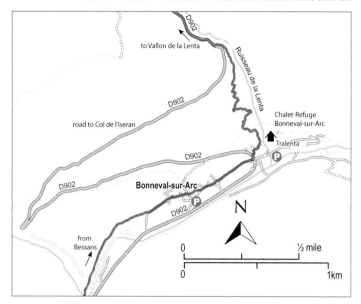

times, but the natural pigments used have faded with time, and now only one animal can be recognised. Information panels beside the track provide details.

A short distance beyond the Rocher du Château, the track ends at a small stream but a footpath continues from it, passing through yet more fine meadows as the valley opens in a long and gentle curve to the northeast. Without diverting from it, you come to **Bonneval-sur-Arc (4hr 30min)**.

Bonneval-sur-Arc (1810m): Together with the neighbouring hamlet of Tralenta, 500 metres further upvalley across the D902 road, the village has a limited range of shops, bars and restaurants, a post office and a tourist office (tel 04 79 05 95 95). There's a *gîte d'étape* in the village square, **Auberge d'Oul** (tel 04 79 05 87 99), with 24 places. In Tralenta, near the tourist office, there's the FFCAM-owned **Chalet-Refuge Bonneval-sur-Arc** (tel 04 78 42 09 17, https://chaletbonnevalsurarc.ffcam.fr/reservation.html), with 15 dormitory places; note that the refuge was unmanned at times and restricted numbers in summer 2021 due to COVID-19.

Hotel accommodation is limited to **Hôtel Le Glacier des Évettes** (tel 04 79 05 94 06), but there are several chalets: **La Bergerie** (tel 04 79 05 95 22); **La Marmotte** (tel 04 79 05 94 82); and **La Pastourelle** (tel 04 79 05 81 56). The village is linked by a daily bus service with Modane and the other villages of the Arc valley.

BONNEVAL AND L'ÉCOT

The attractive gîte at Bonneval makes a good lunch and overnight stop

Bonneval is a delight of well-kept medieval stone houses huddled one against another at the foot of the steeply sloping hillside on the west bank of the Arc. Varnished balconies hung with geraniums and petunias bring colour to the narrow streets; arched doorways and a jigsaw puzzle of stone-slab roofs, stained here and there with rust-coloured lichens, provide a timeless quality – there are no external television aerials or electricity cables to suggest a modern world, and visitors' cars are banned from the centre of the village. But in some respects Bonneval is almost too perfect, and as it has been preserved very much as a showcase it attracts hordes of tourists. A night spent here makes a very pleasant interlude on the Tour of the Vanoise.

Beyond Bonneval and Tralenta, the restored hamlet of L'Écot is the highest in the Haute-Maurienne. Above it, to the southeast, glacier-hung peaks form the Italian frontier. Some good walking country exists on the slopes below the glaciers, with the FFCAM-owned Refuge des Évettes on the Plan des Évettes providing accommodation for walkers and climbers at 2590m, backed by l'Albaron and Ciamarella.

Start	Bonneval-sur-Arc (1810m)
Finish	Val d'Isère (1810m)
Distance	14.5km (variant via Col des Fours: 18km)
Ascent	980m (variant: 1200m)
Descent	980m (variant: 1200m)
Time	5hr 30min (variant: 6hr 30min)
High point	Col de l'Iseran (2764m) (variant via Col des Fours: 2976m)
Facilities	Val d'Isère (5hr 30min) – hotels, camping; the variant goes via Refuge du Fond des Fours (4hr 45min) – PNV refuge

The crossing of Col de l'Iseran marks a transition from the Maurienne to the Tarentaise. South of the col, the Arc river collects the melt of various snowfields and glaciers of the massif, and drains clockwise round the Vanoise block, while north of the Iseran all streams flow into the Isère, a major tributary of the Rhône, in its counterclockwise journey out of the mountains. East of Chambéry. the Arc and Isère join forces, the two rivers effectively containing the Vanoise massif in their caliper-like embrace.

Col de l'Iseran is not only the lynchpin that connects the Maurienne and Tarentaise, it is also a symbol of two contrasting, and sometimes conflicting, styles of mountain usage. From Modane to the col, the Tour of the Vanoise has travelled through country largely unchallenged by the modern world. In the main, refuges provide the only concession to tourist activity, the mountains remaining for the most part unscarred. But from the summit of Col de l'Iseran to Val d'Isère, and beyond through Tignes le Lac and Val Claret, the winter ski industry is much in evidence in some of the hills and valleys. Pylons carrying cableways and ski tows march across the mountains, and broad bulldozed pistes cut a swathe through the hillsides. In spite of this, sections of this land are contained within the Réserve Naturelle de Val d'Isère.

Happily, this stage of the walk is not entirely dominated by the ski industry. Indeed, the first half of the day's route goes through as lovely a valley as any on the tour. Vallon de la Lenta is a delight of gentle pastures, old stone chalets, clear-running streams, a booming cascade – and magnificent views back to the south. There follows a climb through its upper gorge, then out to steep grass slopes that lead to the Col de l'Iseran. The col is crossed by road, and the descent on the northern side shortcuts a few hairpin bends before working a way down ski slopes in the Vallon de l'Iseran. Then the trail turns away from the line of ski tows and gondola lifts to find a zigzag route down through forest to Val d'Isère. It's a challenging day, and a rewarding one.

The alternative branches off the main route after the Vallon de la Lenta climb has been made. It heads into wild territory on the Col des Fours before dropping down to a well-sited refuge and making the long descent into Val d'Isère, adding an hour to the stage while avoiding the ski industry until the outskirts of the town. It is highly recommended in good weather, but in poor visibility or if there's a lot of high snow around, it may be better to stay on the main route.

A few paces above the tourist office in Tralenta (the northeastern end of Bonneval), leave the Iseran road and bear right along a narrow service road. This becomes a track which climbs above the village, and when the track ends you continue straight up the slope on a narrow path, then left alongside a drystone wall. You then twist up the steep hillside, with views onto Bonneval and through the valley growing more extensive as height is gained. Come to a crossing track by a tunnel entrance and continue uphill on the left-hand side of the tunnel. Follow the path as it climbs along the side of a ravine and eventually brings you onto the Iseran road.

Walk along the road for about 1km until it curves sharply to the right over the Pont de la Lenta (2143m, **1hr**). Immediately over the bridge, bear left on a track and wander through the **Vallon de la Lenta**, a beautiful valley dotted with stone chalets and with an impressive waterfall bursting from a rocky cleft ahead. Five minutes along the track, come to a junction with the GR5, where a sign gives 1hr 15min to Pont de la Neige. (The left-hand path is a direct GR5 route from Le Villaron.) Continue heading upvalley towards the waterfall, where the path rises up the right-hand side of the cascades and offers superb views back through the valley to l'Albaron (3637m) and La Grande Ciamarella (3676m), and the glaciers whose melt is the main source of the Arc river.

Above the waterfall, the trail crosses an enclosed pastureland before climbing to the road again at a hairpin bend by an abandoned three-storey building (**Pied Montet**, 2274m). Leave the road and pass alongside the building, where the trail divides. Choose either path, for they rejoin soon after, entering a small gorge and

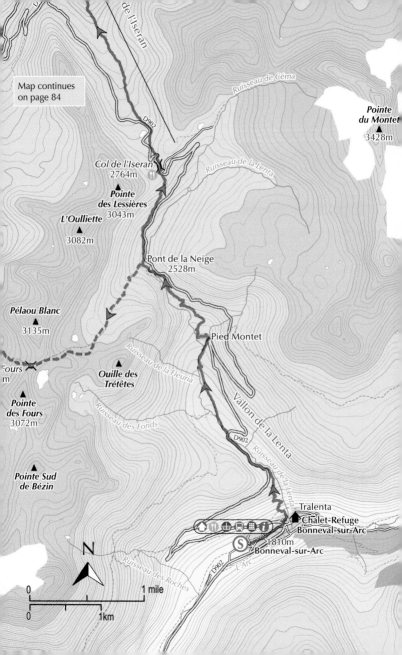

Map continues
on page 84

Ruisseau de l'Iseran

D902

Ruisseau de Céma

**Pointe
du Montet**
3428m

Ruisseau de la Lenta

Col de l'Iseran
2764m

**Pointe
des Lessières**
3043m

L'Oulliette
3082m

Pont de la Neige
2528m

Pélaou Blanc
3135m

Pied Montet

Ruisseau de la Fleuria

Fours
m

**Ouille des
Trétêtes**

Vallon de la Lenta

**Pointe
des Fours**
3072m

Ruisseau des Fonds

D902

Ruisseau de la Lenta

**Pointe Sud
de Bézin**

Tralenta
**Chalet-Refuge
Bonneval=sur-Arc**

S

1810m
Bonneval-sur-Arc

Ruisseau des Roches

D902

L'Arc

N

0   1 mile

0   1km

climbing from one grassy bluff to the next, with spectacular views to the south. Within the gorge, a natural snow bridge spills across the stream. In the past, the route used this to cross the gorge to its left-hand (western) side, but a better path has been made which now slants uphill across the eastern slope. Near the head of the gorge, this path is narrow and exposed, but a length of fixed chain has been provided to safeguard the route. Shortly after, cross to the left side of the stream by a footbridge and come to **Pont de la Neige** (2528m, **2hr 45min**) and a small parking area. The route to Col de l'Iseran continues ahead, just above the road. (Before the parking area, a path junction is signed left to the Col des Fours: this alternative route to Val d'Isère is outlined at the end of this stage.)

PONT DE LA NEIGE

The footbridge near Pont de la Neige spans the Ruisseau de la Lenta at its narrowest point, where it has been channelled through the limestone at the very head of the Lenta gorge. Above Pont de la Neige, an open basin of grassland acts as a catchment for the run-off of several 3000m mountains, their streams gathering momentum in the Ruisseau de Céma which becomes the Ruisseau de la Lenta at the Pont de la Neige. *Bouquetin* can often be seen in the wild upper reaches of the Lenta gorge, where the landscape is in total contrast to that of the vast grassland that feeds it.

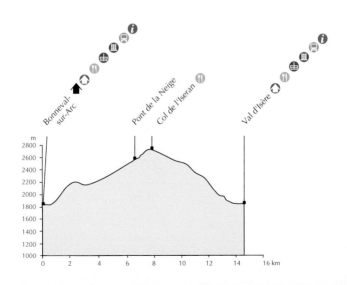

The Vallon de la Lenta

The left-hand trail from the signed junction climbs through a narrow hanging valley to gain the **Col des Fours** (2976m), accessing a mountain wilderness high above Val d'Isère. South of the col, **Pointe des Fours** (3072m) offers a popular and not difficult ascent in 2hr from Pont de la Neige. Although this peak cannot be seen from the path junction near Pont de la Neige, a good view may be had of it from the continuing path on the route to Col de l'Iseran.

Climbing above the road, the gradient of the GR5 path is quite severe at times, but the way is clear, though narrow in places. About 45min from the signed junction near Pont de la Neige, you strike up a final steep grass slope to emerge on the **Col de l'Iseran** (2764m, **3hr 30min**).

Marked by a huge cairn, **Col de l'Iseran** is the highest major road pass in the French Alps. Opened to traffic in 1936, it enjoys extensive views and, on summer days, is often crowded with motor-borne tourists – in stark contrast to all other cols crossed on the Tour of the Vanoise. A chapel (built in 1939) stands just below the road near a rather uninspiring building which houses the inevitable bar-restaurant, souvenirs and tourist information.

Southwest of the col, the obvious sharp peak of **Pointe des Lessières** (3043m) provides a spectacular viewpoint. A route climbs directly to it from the col and comprises sections of path, some minor scrambling and one fixed-rope section.

Cross the road and take a waymarked path that rises a little to pass alongside a small stone hut. You then descend northwestward, crossing the road two or

83

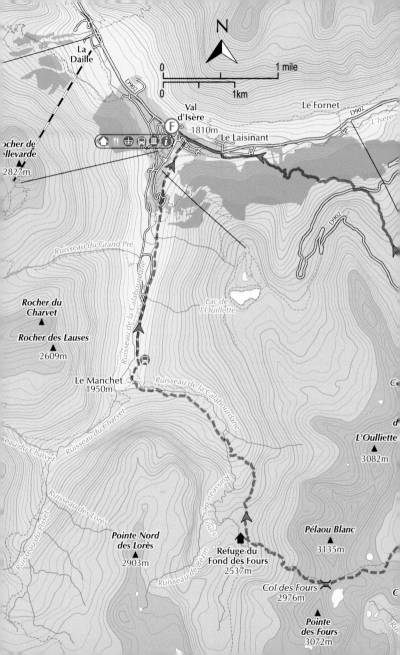

three times and keeping to the right of a small reservoir, before leaving the road altogether by wandering down a piste on the right of a stream in the Vallon de l'Iseran. The route is guided by a variety of pylons and some very large cairns, or stone pyramids, before you leave the piste and cross the stream on a footbridge.

The trail then cuts through rough pastures, curves leftward and drops to the road. About 50 metres up the road, the continuing path descends on the right, soon giving views of Val d'Isère far below. On the northern side of the valley, the ridge linking Grande Sassière, Pointe de la Traversière and Tsanteleina carries the Italian frontier, beyond which lies the Gran Paradiso National Park.

Crossing steep grass- and shrub-covered slopes, the way then descends through larchwoods on a twisting path. There are several junctions in this woodland, but the route to Val d'Isère is obvious and signed. Near the foot of the slope, cross a footbridge over a torrent, and soon after this pass through the small hamlet of **Le Laisinant** (1855m) – a 'suburb' of Val d'Isère. There are some attractive buildings here. Staying on the south side of the valley, the path takes you past them, then above a campsite, and eventually brings you into one of the most prestigious ski resorts of the French Alps (**5hr 30min**).

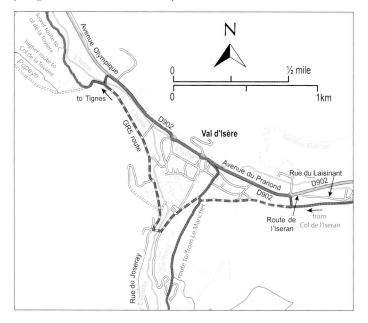

Val d'Isère (1810m) has all services including dentist, pharmacies, PO, plenty of shops, restaurants, bars, banks with ATMs, and a tourist office (tel 04 79 06 06 60). Among the lower-priced hotels still open in summer, try **Les Crêtes Blanches** (tel 04 79 06 05 45). The campsite in Le Laisinant, **Camping Les Richardes** (tel 06 95 36 20 40), is open from mid June to mid September. A bus service runs from Val d'Isère to Bourg-St-Maurice for SNCF trains.

VAL D'ISÈRE

With abundant snow cover in winter, Val d'Isère is primarily a ski resort – and a fashionable one at that – but it also attracts visitors in summer, although a number of hotels are operational in winter only. By contrast with neighbouring Tignes le Lac and Val Claret, the town's modern architecture largely follows traditional lines. In her 1930s memoir, *Mountain Holidays*, Janet Adam Smith's description of Val d'Isère included a 'huddle of carts, outhouses, washing, hens, timber, and children'; while in his guide to the Alps published in 1939, that Alpine connoisseur RLG Irving listed Val d'Isère as the second of his favourite centres in the Graian Alps, giving as his criteria 'altitude, good quarters, green pastures, streams, flowers, and plenty of peaks to look at as well as to climb' (*The Alps*, published by Batsford, 1939). Of course, Irving was writing about a Val d'Isère he would hardly recognise today, although much of his listed criteria remains good.

The abundance of mechanical uplift is something neither Irving nor Janet Adam Smith would have known, yet it has enabled tens of thousands of visitors to enjoy scenes that previously would have been the preserve only of climbers and hardened hillwalkers. Immediately above the town to the west, for example, and accessible by both *téléphérique* (cable car) from Val d'Isère and the Funival (funicular railway) from La Daille, the Rocher de Bellevarde (2827m) is a noted viewpoint and major ski venue. The summit panorama embraces the Isère valley, the frontier range of the Grande Sassière, Tsanteleina, the Grande Aiguille Rousse and the Glacier des Sources de l'Isère, with Mont Blanc to the north and all the main summits of the Vanoise massif to the south and west.

Alternative route to Val d'Isère via the Col des Fours
This route takes an hour longer and involves more climbing than the main route but, as it avoids the Col de l'Iseran and the descent affected by the ski industry, it is a much better walk in good weather conditions and makes for a great day in the high mountains. It crosses both the remains of glaciers long since disappeared

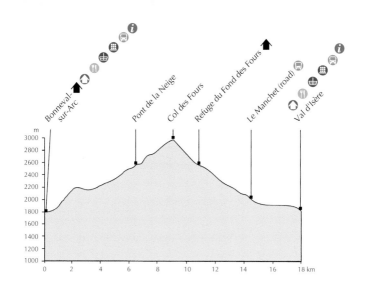

and a high remote col, so is probably best avoided in poor weather. (Total stage distance: 18km; ascent and descent: 1200m; total stage time: 6hr 30min.)

Take the main route to the **Pont de la Neige** road bridge (2528m, **2hr 45min**). At a path junction before the parking area, turn left, initially southwest, into terrain devoid of grass, signed to the Col des Fours. The views back to the grassy slopes of the Col de l'Iseran contrast with the rocky wilderness ahead. The path

The stony path climbs towards the Col des Fours

The road and path snake towards the Col de l'Iseran, seen from the path above Pont de la Neige

crosses the rubble of the ancient Glacier de la Jave, perhaps a sign of how the mountains will look if glaciers melt further. After a first ridge, traverse above a high tarn to the **Col des Fours** (2976m, **4hr 15min**). From the col, descend steeply to the **Refuge du Fond des Fours** (**4hr 45min**), turning right (north) at the 2542m path junction from which the refuge is clearly visible.

> **Refuge du Fond des Fours** (2537m, tel 06 03 54 50 55): The refuge is on the lip of the hanging valley, with spectacular views north towards Val d'Isère and the Sassière mountain range behind. As it is likely to be reached around lunchtime, it makes an enviable stopping point, so beautiful you may well wonder why bother to continue the descent.

From the refuge, descend north. As the hut is a convenient lunch destination for day-walkers, the path is good, descending rocky drops, levelling out and descending steeply again. Across the valley, a couple of mountain inns make inviting stops. The path joins a track and descends to the river then to a road at **Le Manchet** (1950m, **5hr 45min**). There are summer buses down the road into Val d'Isère from here, if desired.

The path continues for 1.5km along the quiet road, then, after passing pony-trekking and other sports facilities on the left, the road falls away and a good path continues to Val d'Isère. Pass outlying chalets at La Légettaz, then on open ground under a series of ski lifts to make your way into the centre of **Val d'Isère** (1810m, **6hr 30min**).

STAGE 7A
Bonneval-sur-Arc to Refuge de la Femma

Start	Bonneval-sur-Arc (1810m)
Finish	Refuge de la Femma (2352m)
Distance	20km
Ascent	1610m
Descent	1070m
Time	8hr
High point	Col des Fours (2976m); Col de la Rocheure (2911m)
Facilities	Refuge du Fond des Fours (4hr 45min) – PNV refuge; Refuge de la Femma (8hr) – PNV refuge + camping

This high, remote and wild option provides a great but challenging day that avoids all ski and other industry around Val d'Isère and Tignes. It should only be taken in good conditions. The climb to the Col des Fours is almost entirely waymarked but there are some remote and rocky sections where the waymarking becomes less clear. The crossing to the Col de la Rocheure is other-worldly, far removed from the towns below. The higher part of the route is occasionally unclear but large cairns point the way. If visibility is poor and the cairns cannot be seen, it would be better to turn back and drop down to the Refuge du Fond des Fours and Val d'Isère. The final descent to the Femma refuge is straightforward, and clearly marked.

Follow Stage 7 to the **Pont de la Neige** (2528m, **2hr 45min**), then take the Stage 7 alternative route via the **Col des Fours** (2976m, **4hr 15min**) and onwards to reach the **2542m path junction** above Refuge du Fond des Fours. The refuge is clearly visible 200 metres north. Turn right to visit it.

> **Refuge du Fond des Fours** (2537m, tel 06 03 54 50 55): The refuge is likely to be reached around lunchtime and is close enough that it works as a lunch or refreshment stop, although the remote site and magnificent views north to the Sassière range mean you may well be tempted to linger.

From the 2542m junction, turn left, heading south. Climb alongside a stream and cross a wide glacial bowl, then climb steeply to a small col in the ridge (Col

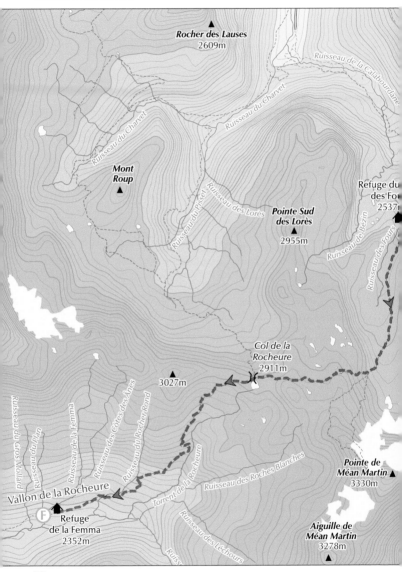

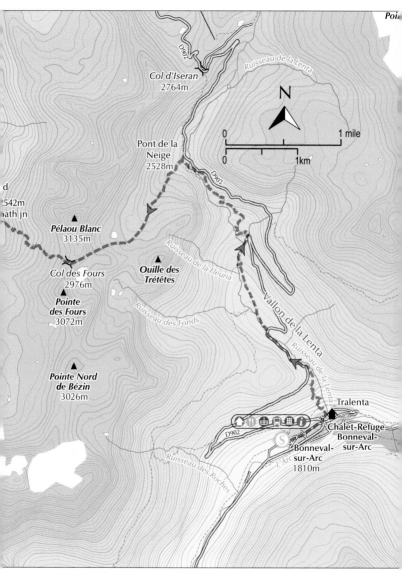

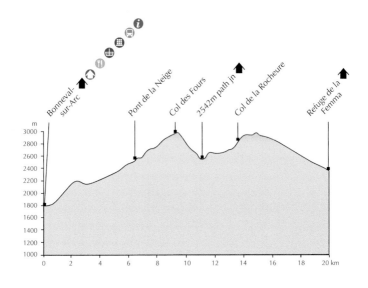

de Bézin, 2929m). Keep a careful eye open for painted waymarks here, for this is where it is easiest to lose the trail. Large cairns also mark the way across a desert

Col de la Rocheure and the small cold tarn on the south side

Wild country on the route to the Col de la Rocheure

of stones, until you eventually emerge at the **Col de la Rocheure** (2911m, **6hr 45min**).

The mountain route from Val d'Isère joins here (see Stage 8A); it is not a busy crossing but you are likely to meet walkers for the first time in some hours. The tarn below the col looks cold but beautiful, with a backdrop formed by the snow-and-rock mountain of the Pointe de Méan Martin and the northern side of the wall of mountains that you have only previously seen from the Arc valley in the south.

The descent is clearly marked on a good path. Pass the cold-looking tarn just below the col and drop through stony terrain that becomes increasingly grassy. **Refuge de la Femma** (**8hr**) is reached as the route levels out.

> **Refuge de la Femma** (2532m, tel 04 79 05 45 40): Owned by the PNV, this timber-built refuge consists of three buildings, similar in design to the Refuge de la Leisse on the main route. It has 64 dormitory places and a full meals service with a *gardien* in residence from mid June to late September, but at other times the winter room is permanently open with 24 beds. A single overnight's camping is permitted for a small fee.

STAGE 8
Val d'Isère to Refuge de la Leisse

Start	Val d'Isère (1810m)
Finish	Refuge de la Leisse (2487m)
Distance	18.5km (high-level variant: 17km)
Ascent	1190m (variant: 1230m)
Descent	500m (variant: 550m)
Time	7hr (variant: 7hr)
High point	Col de la Leisse (2729m) (variant via the Tovière: 2695m)
Facilities	Tignes le Lac (3hr) – hotels; Val Claret (3hr 30min) – hotels; Refuge de la Leisse (7hr) – PNV refuge + camping

With two cols to cross (Pas de la Tovière and Col de la Leisse), it will be apparent that this stage, which returns the trek to mountain wilderness, could be challenging. But having walked this far along the Tour of the Vanoise and tackled steeper gradients than those demanded by either of these crossings, under normal summer conditions most trekkers will take it in their stride.

This is another stage divided into two distinct parts. The morning will be spent in view either of major ski resorts or of their mechanical accoutrements (or both), while the second half leads into a landscape with more remote appeal. From Val d'Isère, the way climbs through forest and along gently rising grassland to gain the 2267m Pas de la Tovière, from where it is possible to see Mont Blanc in the distance. Descent is then made to the ski resort of Tignes le Lac, but this is quickly passed on the way to Val Claret – an equally obtrusive resort of high-rise buildings completely out of keeping with the landscape.

Happily, the trail soon works a way into an untamed land of big mountains, the highest of which is La Grande Motte, whose snowfields and glaciers shine like mirrors in the sunlight. La Grande Motte rises immediately above Col de la Leisse, its long southwesterly wall plunging into the valley in which Refuge de la Leisse is located. On the way to it, the trail descends to moody tarns, screes and boulderscapes loud with the call of marmots.

From Val Claret onward, all the way to Modane, the Tour of the Vanoise follows the route of the GR55, a high mountain alternative to the GR5, continuing to Pralognan and Modane. This gives a scenically varied and spectacular five-day trek to match the grandeur experienced during the

Maurienne half of the tour as far as Val d'Isère. (See Short tour 3: Traverse of the Vanoise.)

There are two alternatives worth considering, both of which avoid the visual intrusion of Tignes le Lac and Val Claret. The first of these options (described below as a variant to this stage) crosses the Tovière and Fresse mountains above the Charvet valley south of Val d'Isère, then rejoins GR55 and the main route to Col de la Leisse. The second alternative (described below as Stage 8A) goes to the head of the Charvet valley, crosses the 2911m Col de la Rocheure and descends to Refuge de la Femma. The following day (Stage 9A) takes you down the Vallon de la Rocheure and via Refuge Entre Deux Eaux to join the main route from Refuge de la Leisse (Stage 9) at the Pont de Croé-Vie before heading to the Col de la Vanoise.

Walk through Val d'Isère along the main road (D902) heading northwest towards La Daille and Tignes. On the outskirts of town, just after a Spar supermarket and filling station, turn left into a minor road by a large building named L'Aigle Blanc. Over the Isère river, bear right on a track which curves left by a large electricity building. A footpath runs alongside the track among larch trees, goes behind the electricity building, and across a stream joins another track.

The GR5 route here has been rerouted for some years, perhaps permanently. Follow the path to **La Daille (30min)** and then climb steeply, first across a piste and then up a wooded path to a **2020m path junction**.

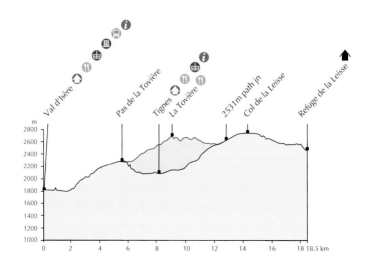

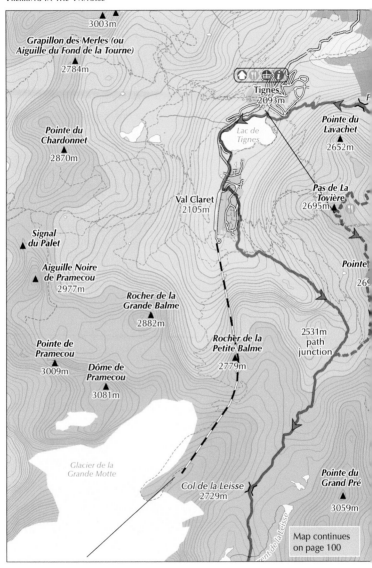

3003m

Grapillon des Merles (ou
Aiguille du Fond de la Tourne)
2784m

Pointe du
Chardonnet
2870m

Tignes
2093m

Lac de
Tignes

Pointe du
Lavachet
2652m

Signal
du Palet

Val Claret
2105m

Pas de La
Tovière
2695m

Aiguille Noire
de Pramecou
2977m

Rocher de la
Grande Balme
2882m

Pointe
26

Pointe de
Pramecou
3009m

Rocher de la
Petite Balme
2779m

2531m
path
junction

Dôme de
Pramecou
3081m

Glacier de la
Grande Motte

Col de la Leisse
2729m

Pointe du
Grand Pré
3059m

Map continues
on page 100

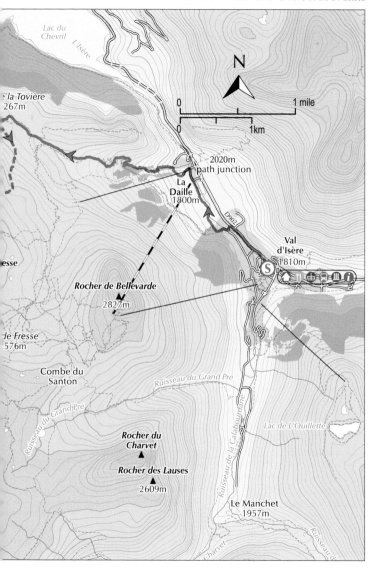

97

There are several signed junctions as you follow the trail out of the trees and up into the Vallon de la Tovière – a gentle, pastoral valley walled on the left by Pointe du Lavachet (2652m) and on the right by the crags of Roc de la Tovière.

The walk through the Tovière valley is easy and undemanding. Marmots abound, and as you approach the saddle at its head (**Pas de la Tovière, 2hr 30min**), you wander alongside a grass airstrip which belongs to the Val d'Isère Flying Club.

> The **Pas de la Tovière** (2267m) is a broad saddle of grass, rocks and flowers. From here, Mont Blanc can be seen on a clear day, while far below lies the dammed Lac du Chevril. Behind the lake, another valley cuts into the walling mountains, within which lies the Réserve Naturelle de la Grande Sassière.

As the path continues, now descending westward, the high-rise buildings of Tignes le Lac appear in the valley below; the architecture of this purpose-built ski resort seems completely out of place with the setting, while its cableways lace the mountainsides on both flanks of the valley. The trail takes you directly down to the edge of the village, but although the GR5 enters Tignes, it's unnecessary to go that way unless you need refreshments or supplies. For these, take the main path into **Tignes le Lac** (**3hr**).

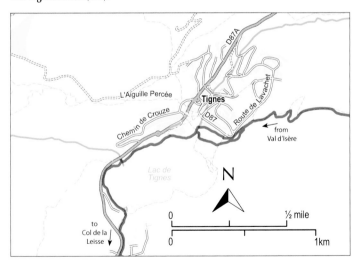

Tignes le Lac (2093m): While much of the accommodation here is closed in summer, several hotels remain open. There are also shops, bars, restaurants, a PO and tourist information (tel 04 79 40 04 40).

TIGNES LE LAC

The original village of Tignes was located in the Isère valley below La Daille, but this was flooded in the 1950s when the dam was built to create Lac du Chevril. Its ultra-modern replacement grew alongside Lac de Tignes to exploit the area's ski potential. Linked with Val d'Isère's 'Espace Killy', there are now more than 300km of pistes and over 100 lifts, including an underground funicular that transports skiers from neighbouring Val Claret to a panoramic restaurant at over 3000m on the Grande Motte's glacier. From there, a large *téléphérique* (cable car) carries passengers to a point just below the summit of La Grande Motte at 3450m. Despite this development (and the fact that it is used for year-round skiing), the Glacier de la Grande Motte has been dubbed the Réserve Naturelle de Tignes.

In winter, the resort caters for more than 20,000 visitors at a time. Fortunately, that number is greatly reduced in summer, when much of the accommodation is closed. The lake, which is its most attractive feature, is a natural one which once lay in a treeless basin of high pasture but is now the focus of a variety of water sports.

The Tour of the Vanoise ignores Tignes le Lac as much as possible and takes the broad gravel path round the left-hand (east) shore of the lake. At the far end, continue alongside a golf course, then beside a road heading towards more high-rise buildings in **Val Claret** (**3hr 30min**).

Val Claret (2105m): Like neighbouring Tignes le Lac, most of Val Claret's accommodation is closed in summer, although it has shops, bars, a bank and tourist information that may remain open.

On coming to a roundabout, turn left then cross the road to a continuing gravel path slanting left below some of the high-rise buildings. A few red-and-white waymarks will be seen. Passing below the buildings, come onto a road and turn right. When it forks, bear left (keep ahead if you need refreshments). Turn right, then cross the road, go up a slope and bear right, soon coming to a footpath (GR55) behind Val Claret. A signpost here gives directions to several destinations, including Col de la Leisse (in 1hr 55min) and Refuge de la Leisse (in 3hr).

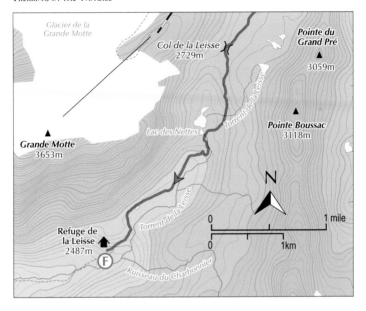

The path angles round the hillside and goes beneath a chairlift, then up a slope along the line of the lift, eventually coming onto a track/piste where you bear right, continuing uphill. Keep alert for a narrow path on the right, which guides you away from the track to pass along the line of the chairlift once more. (This chairlift goes almost as far as the Col de Fresse.) Cutting across a steep slope, the path passes beneath the lift then goes up through a grassy gully and across open grassland. The high-level variant over the Fresse (described below) rejoins at the **2531m path junction (5hr 15min)**.

The landscape becomes more enticing now that mechanical intrusion has been left behind, and as you enter the national park once more the glacier-capped Grande Motte dominates the view ahead. A sign now indicates 1hr 15min to Col de la Leisse. In normal summer conditions, the trail is clearly defined, but when remnants of winter's snow remain, or following a recent snowfall, concentration will be required to keep along the line of the few cairns that guide the way. Climbing over a series of false cols, you come onto the **Col de la Leisse**, a fine, wild little pass (2729m, **6hr**).

On the south side of the col, the trail goes through a rocky trough, before sloping down a series of natural steps in an untamed and majestic region of rock

A cold and snowy crossing of the Col de la Leisse in early September

and grass below the cliffs and screes of La Grande Motte. Wander along the eastern side of **Lac des Nettes**, then descend to the Plan des Nettes. At the far end of a small intermittent lake, a tiny barrage has been built across its outflow, and the trail brings you round towards the dam, then descends again to the **Refuge de la Leisse (7hr)**.

> **Refuge de la Leisse** (2487m, tel 09 72 40 03 23, out of season tel 06 15 44 33 68): Owned by the PNV, the refuge consists of three tent-shaped timber buildings standing on a spur of land overlooking the lower Vallon de la Leisse. It has 32 dormitory places, plus space for camping, a full meals service, and self-catering facilities. Although it has showers, the toilet and washing facilities are somewhat limited. A *gardien* is usually in residence from mid June to mid September.
>
> Both the situation and outlook of the refuge are very fine, and its remoteness helps to create a convivial atmosphere in the dining room, especially on cold evenings. Marmot and chamois can frequently be seen nearby.

High-level route to Refuge de la Leisse by the Tovière

At 17km, this option is slightly shorter than the main route, but the walking time (around 7hr) is the same. Although it is impossible to avoid the ski industry

Looking back along the entrancing Pointe de Fresse ridge

entirely, this is an interesting variant with fantastic 360-degree views under good weather conditions. Yes, there are ski slopes and a station right at the summit of the Tovière, but these do not intrude before then and are quickly passed. The high-level traverse over the ridge of the Pointe de Fresse makes this a more challenging day than the lower route; the ridge is reasonably broad, but should be avoided on a windy day or in poor visibility, in which case the main Tignes route is best. If you wish to bail out, it is possible to take the cable car down to Tignes and continue on the main route. This variant joins the main route after the Col de Fresse.

Follow Stage 8 as described above from Val d'Isère to **Pas de la Tovière** (2267m, **2hr 30min**). From the broad saddle, find a path heading back southeast. There are many more paths hereabouts than are shown on the map, and they are well signed. The traverse steepens, climbs a gully, crosses one stream then another, and continues climbing close to a ski lift. Take a ski road to reach the ridge and then climb another piste directly to the summit of the **Tovière** (2695m, **4hr 15min**). This last section is steep and frankly a bit unpleasant, but it is only 15 minutes to the summit.

Pass through the ski station (refreshments available) and descend steeply for 5min to a col, and then climb the wide path towards the **Pointe de Fresse** (2694m, **4hr 45min**). The ridge narrows and passes several tops before the Pointe (which is probably not the highest top on the ridge), avoiding the ridgeline in places. An hour after leaving the Tovière, the path drops down to the Col de Fresse (2576m).

From the col, drop southwest to join the GR55 at the **2531m path junction** (**5hr 15min**), following the main route (as described above) for the rest of this stage via **Col de la Leisse** (2729m, **6hr**) to **Refuge de la Leisse** (2487m, **7hr**).

STAGE 8A
Val d'Isère to Refuge de la Femma

Start	Val d'Isère (1810m)
Finish	Refuge de la Femma (2352m)
Distance	18km
Ascent	1290m
Descent	750m
Time	7hr
High point	Col de la Rocheure (2911m)
Facilities	Refuge de la Femma (7hr) – PNV refuge

This is a high mountain crossing and, although well waymarked, is best saved for a good day, as the path to the Col de la Rocheure at over 2900m is steep, stony and remote. Navigation under poor conditions would be a challenge. It is a matter of wonder that this area has escaped the ski industry to remain a mountain wilderness.

There are two ways around the Rocher du Mont Roup, both excellent, the circular tour of Mont Roup being a waymarked and popular trail for day-walkers in Val d'Isère. There are no facilities after leaving the valley. The final descent from the col to Refuge de la Femma is straightforward.

From the centre of Val d'Isère, follow signs for the Refuge du Fond des Fours and the Mont Roup path south into the Calabourdane valley. Pass under ski lifts and through a final burst of chalets and come into the wide and pleasant valley. There are pony-trekking and other sports facilities across the river. Reach the roadhead at **Le Manchet** (1950m, **1hr 15min**).

Drop down across the river, pass a flat grassy area where cattle assemble, and cross then climb gradually alongside the **Ruisseau du Charvet** for a further 2km to a **2124m path junction** (**2hr**). From here, there are two possible routes around Mont Roup.

The east side of Mont Roup
For a shorter route on the eastern flank of Mont Roup, keep left at the junction, pass the last farm (**Chalet du Riondet**) and climb steadily on the grassy path to

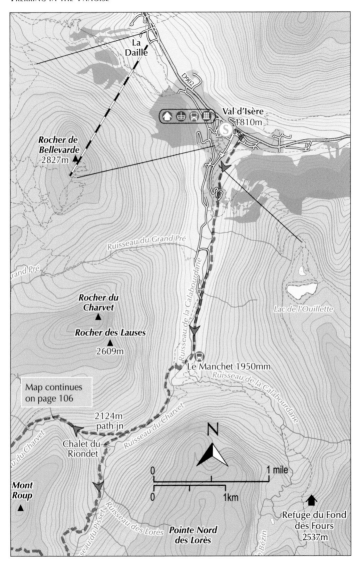

La Daille

D902

⌂ 🏛 🚌 🏨 Val d'Isère
1810m

Ⓢ

Rocher de Bellevarde
2827m ▲

Ruisseau du Grand Pré

Grand Pré

Rocher du Charvet ▲

Rocher des Lauses ▲
2609m

Ruisseau de la Calaboudane

Lac de l'Ouillette

Le Manchet 1950mm

Ruisseau de la Calaboudane

Map continues
on page 106

2124m
path jn

Ruisseau du Charvet

Chalet du Riondet

N

Mont Roup ▲

0 ——————— 1 mile

0 ——————— 1km

Ruisseau du Piset

Ruisseau des Lorès

Pointe Nord des Lorès

Bézin

Refuge du Fond des Fours
2537m ▲

104

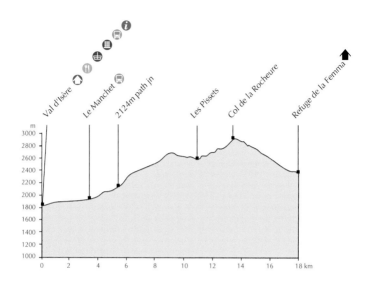

reach the tarn at **Les Pissets** (2580m). This route saves about 1hr 30min, and 150m of up and down.

The west side of Mont Roup

The longer circuit on the west side of Mont Roup keeps right at the 2124m junction. The path sweeps right, then left, and climbs steadily under the cliffs on Mont Roup's north face. Turning southeast, it crosses a very pleasant, undulating and grassy tarned area popular with cattle, before dropping 100m to meet the shorter route at **Les Pissets** (2580m, **4hr 30min**).

From Les Pissets, the ascent to the col is signed and waymarked. It climbs a steep rise then meanders through glacial debris before steepening for the final stony climb to the **Col de la Rocheure** (2911m, **5hr 45min**). This section feels – and is – wild and remote, with only rocky mountains and stony ground for company.

The view from the col to the high ridge running from the Pointe de Méan Martin, Pointes du Châtelard and the Grand Roc Noir is wild. At 'only' 3300–3500m high, the ridge looks challenging, although the *voies normales* (normal climbing routes) are straightforward Alpine rock climbs at easier grades (around PD, *peu difficile*).

105

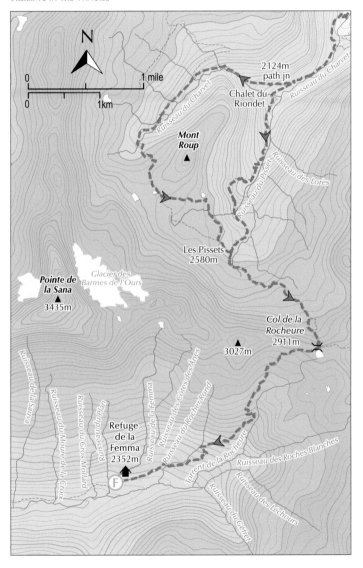

Looking south to the Méan Martin from the Col de la Rocheure

The descent is clearly marked on a good path. Pass the photogenic but cold-looking tarn just below the col, then descend through stony terrain that becomes increasingly grassy. The **Refuge de la Femma** is reached as the route levels out (**7hr**).

> **Refuge de la Femma** (2352m, tel 04 79 05 45 40): Owned by the PNV, the refuge is timber-built and consists of three buildings, similar in design to the Refuge de la Leisse. It has 64 dormitory places plus a designated space for overnight camping, a full meals service and kitchen facilities. A *gardien* is in residence from mid June to late September, but at other times the winter room is permanently open with 24 beds.

STAGE 9
Refuge de la Leisse to Pralognan-la-Vanoise

Start	Refuge de la Leisse (2487m)
Finish	Pralognan-la-Vanoise (1420m)
Distance	18km
Ascent	450m
Descent	1520m
Time	6hr
High point	Col de la Vanoise (2517m)
Facilities	Refuge Entre Deux Eaux (1hr 30min + 20min) – privately owned refuge; Refuge du Col de la Vanoise (3hr 30min) – FFCAM refuge; Refuge Les Barmettes (4hr 45min) – privately owned refuge + camping; Pralognan (6hr) – hotels, camping

The crossing of the Col de la Vanoise to Pralognan is a classic stage, passing as it does from a sense of remoteness experienced at La Leisse, via the close proximity of high mountains on the col itself, to the comforts of a low-key resort village hemmed in by lofty peaks. It forms an integral part of the shorter Tour des Glaciers de la Vanoise, and the final section is especially popular with all active (and semi-active) visitors to Pralognan, for whom no summer holiday in the village would be complete without spending at least one day climbing to the col and back again with or without the partial aid of a cableway. It is, quite simply, the best-known walk in the Vanoise Alps.

The day begins with an easy descent through the Vallon de la Leisse to the historic hump-backed Pont de Croé-Vie, followed by a relatively short climb to a high scoop of mountain country under the southwest flanks of Pointe Mathews (a secondary summit of La Grande Casse) leading to the Col de la Vanoise. Over this you descend past towering walls of moraine, cross a shallow lake, then plunge steeply down to Pralognan on trails that will seldom be walked in solitude.

At the high point of this stage, Refuge du Col de la Vanoise is the largest and busiest of all huts on the tour, and although it is reached rather too early in the day to normally consider staying, such is its location – close to glaciers, tarns, rock walls and charismatic peaks – that it would be worth checking in for the night and spending the rest of the day exploring. In this case, it should be feasible to continue to Refuge de Péclet-Polset tomorrow (see Stage 10 for details).

Given spare days, an alternative would be to divert from the main route at Pont de Croé-Vie and head south a short distance to Refuge Entre Deux Eaux, book in for the night and spend the remainder of the day wandering in the Vallon de la Rocheure, which lies roughly parallel to the Vallon de la Leisse. This gives an opportunity to unravel a little more of the district's geography and makes a highly recommended 'rest day'. (See Stage 9A for the route out of the Rocheure valley.)

Leaving Refuge de la Leisse, backtrack a short distance to a signed path junction, then descend southwestward into the lower valley which, below the refuge, is almost flat-bottomed, and a good place to watch marmot, *bouquetin* and chamois. A footbridge takes you across to the left bank of the Torrent de la Leisse, and the path remains on that side of the valley all the way to Pont de Croé-Vie.

Losing height via a series of natural steps, and with several minor streams to cross, the route makes a steady curve to the south. A cascade can be seen ahead, pouring from cliffs that wall the way to Col de la Vanoise. High above, Pointe Mathews is seriously foreshortened, while behind, the Grande Motte appears a very different mountain from the glacial giant that dominated the view from Col de la Leisse.

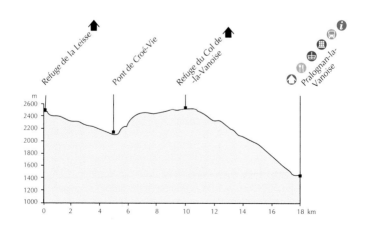

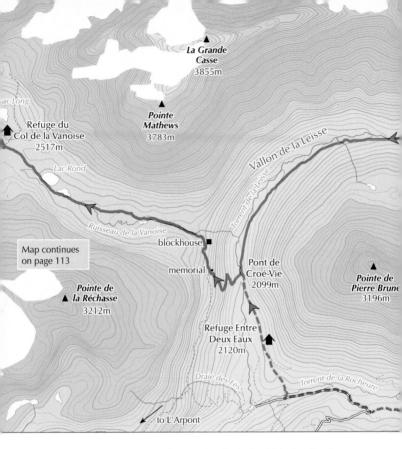

Turning the bend in the valley, peaks which should be familiar from Stage 4 (Arpont to Plan du Lac) appear downstream in the southwest. Come to a path junction by the attractive stone bridge known as the **Pont de Croé-Vie** (2099m, **1hr 15min**). Dating from the 16th century, the bridge originally carried traders over the river on what was then an important salt route between the Maurienne and Tarentaise.

Diversion to Refuge Entre Deux Eaux

To break the stage by diverting to Refuge Entre Deux Eaux (as suggested in Stage 9 introduction), take the path which continues down the left bank from Pont de Croé-Vie, reaching **Refuge Entre Deux Eaux** in 20min from the bridge. Overnighting

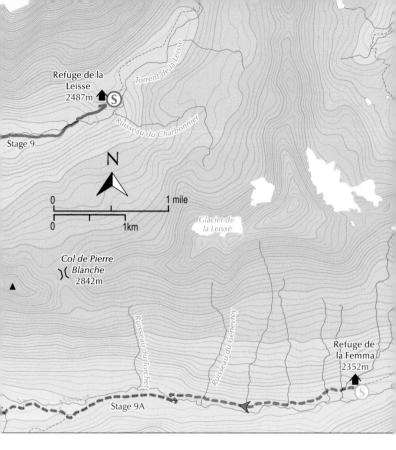

here provides an opportunity to explore the Vallon de la Rocheure, after which you can resume Stage 9 by retracing your steps to the Pont de Croé-Vie.

Refuge Entre Deux Eaux (2120m, tel 04 79 05 27 13): Privately owned, the refuge has 38 dormitory places and a full meals service, and is manned from early June to late September. Just below the refuge, the Alpage Catherine Richard is renowned for its cheese (see www.mons-cheese.co.uk/bleu-de-termignon).

To continue the stage, cross the bridge and begin the ascent to the Col de la Vanoise on a zigzag path; at first flanked by drifts of alpenrose, the terrain becomes

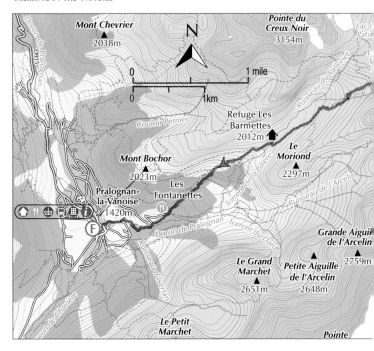

stonier and barer as height is gained. About 45min from the Pont de Croé-Vie, you come to a trail junction where the left fork heads south across the slopes of the Pointe de la Réchasse to join the GR5 along the west side of the Doron gorge. Ignore this option and continue ahead to pass alongside a triangular **memorial stone** erected in memory of two army officers who perished in the mountains.

Just beyond the memorial, the path cuts across a steep slope which, when snow-covered (as it often is well into the summer), is potentially dangerous and will demand care when crossing. Alternatively, skirt below it, then climb the rocks on the far side and pass just to the left of a wartime **blockhouse**; this consists of a series of tunnels, each one opening to a former gun emplacement commanding long views over either the Vallon de la Leisse or the upper reaches of the Doron de Termignon's valley.

The trail continues to rise, but soon eases into an almost level valley lying between Pointe de la Réchasse and Pointe Mathews. Cross the **Ruisseau de la Vanoise** on stepping stones and continue on its north bank. The valley through

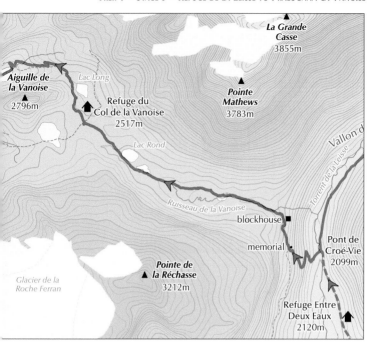

which the path strikes northwestward is marshy in places, but shallow tarns lie elsewhere, and as you draw nearer to the col so the huge screes that spill from Pointe Mathews create a barren spectacle.

Recrossing the stream, cairns direct the way across a stony plain to pass along the left-hand side of a tarn, beyond which you climb a short grass step to overlook **Lac Rond**, with the glaciers of La Grande Casse hanging above the far shore, and the great slabs of Pointe de la Grande Glière and Aiguille de l'Épéna towering ahead to the right. Now cross an open grass plain, on the far side of which stands the substantially rebuilt **Refuge du Col de la Vanoise (3hr 30min)**.

Refuge du Col de la Vanoise (2517m, tel 04 79 08 25 23): FFCAM-owned, the refuge has 129 dormitory places, full meals service and self-catering facilities, and is manned from early March until the end of September. Views are tremendous and dominated by the Grande Casse, below which lies yet another lake, Lac Long. Once again, marmots abound almost everywhere. Despite its

The Grande Casse seen from the stepping stones across Lac des Vaches below the Col de la Vanoise

popularity, the refuge takes on a much calmer character once the daytime visitors have departed.

Paths descend to Pralognan on either side of the Aiguille de la Vanoise, which rises behind the refuge to the west, but the recommended route takes the north flank. Pass along the right-hand side of the refuge, heading a little west of north, and skirt the deep bowl containing **Lac Long**, then in zigzags turn west below the vast rock slabs of the Aiguille. It's impossible to lose the way as it is mostly broad, as befits a mule track, and busy with walkers struggling up from Pralognan. A more direct, and much narrower, trail descends to the left of the main track, but the two converge shortly before reaching the shallow **Lac des Vaches** (2319m), which you cross on a causeway of stone slabs.

From the lake's outflow, another splendid view may be had by looking back to the Grande Casse, its glaciers and vast mounds of moraine debris, and the Aiguille and Pointes de l'Épéna to their left. And when you gaze southwest, the deep valley of the Doron de Chavière, backed by the Dents de la Portetta, provides a strong hint that the remainder of the descent will be a strain on the knees.

Continuing down towards the valley, the trail remains a broad and stony track, but there are several minor paths that suggest alternative options; all are more or less steep and twisting among marmot burrows and low-growing shrubs. Then the main trail is contained between drystone walls, and shortly after crossing the stream and leaving the national park once more, it reaches the privately owned **Refuge Les Barmettes (4hr 45min)**.

> **Refuge Les Barmettes** (2012m, tel 04 79 08 75 64): With 27 dormitory places, the refuge is open from mid June to mid September and there's the possibility of an overnight pitch for campers. Close by is the top station of a cableway from Les Fontanettes.

Below the refuge, where the broad track forks, keep down the track until you come to a building on the edge of forest, where a sign gives this as Dou de l'Ecu (1770m). Leave the track for a forest path just left of the building. This takes you down to a car park, cableway and restaurant at **Les Fontanettes** (1644m), about 45min from Les Barmettes.

Pass along the left side of the restaurant, then bear left on a footpath which descends past a few stone chalets. This comes onto a road at a hairpin bend. Walk round the hairpin, then break away left on the continuing path which enters forest once more. On the way down to Pralognan it's worth making a short diversion on a signed path to a *table d'orientation* (panoramic map), from which you gain an interesting overview of the village and its surrounding mountains. The path continues to twist down to a small chapel, water fountain and a cobbled alley leading into the main street of **Pralognan (6hr)**.

As the path descends, views into the Pralognan valley widen and the route of the next stage is seen

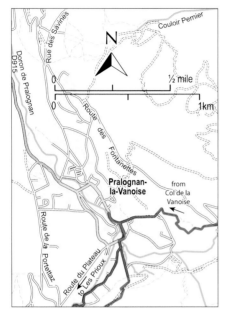

Pralognan-la-Vanoise (1420m): Hemmed in by crowding mountains, Pralognan is a small but lively resort with year-round appeal, but especially in summer when it attracts thousands of walkers, climbers and general tourists by its reputation as one of the finest centres in the Vanoise region. This bustling resort village has a range of shops, bars, restaurants, banks with ATMs, a medical centre, PO, Bureau des Guides (mountain guides bureau), and a tourist office (tel 04 79 08 79 08), which also houses the national park's information bureau (tel 04 79 08 71 49). There's a bus link with Moûtiers for the high-speed TGV train service to Paris.

For lower-priced accommodation, try the **Epicéa Lodge** (tel 04 79 08 73 11) at the Isertan campsite (see below). Pralognan also has several hotels: **La Vallée Blanche** (tel 04 79 08 70 74); **Le Grand Bec** (tel 04 79 08 71 10); **Les Airelles** (tel 04 79 08 70 32); and **La Vanoise** (tel 04 79 08 70 34). In addition, there are two campsites, both of which are open from June to mid September: **Alpes Lodges (Camping Isertan)** (tel 04 79 08 75 24) and **Camping Municipal Le Chamois** (tel 06 59 46 45 34).

STAGE 9A
Refuge de la Femma to Pralognan-la-Vanoise

Start	Refuge de la Femma (2352m)
Finish	Pralognan-la-Vanoise (1420m)
Distance	23km
Ascent	540m
Descent	1470m
Time	7hr
High point	Refuge de la Femma (2352m)
Facilities	Refuge Entre Deux Eaux (2hr) – privately owned refuge; Refuge du Col de la Vanoise (4hr 30min) – FFCAM refuge; Refuge Les Barmettes (5hr 45min) – privately owned refuge + camping; Pralognan (7hr) – hotels, camping

For walkers who have taken one of the high routes to the Refuge de la Femma via Stages 7A and 8A, this link stage brings them back onto the main route, which it joins after a little more than 2hr shortly after passing the privately owned Refuge Entre Deux Eaux. From this point on, Stage 9A follows the main route described in Stage 9. (The entire route of Stage 9A is shown on Stage 9 route map.)

Alternatively, for trekkers with time and the desire, it is worthwhile spending an extra day and visiting the Refuge de la Leisse, overnighting there or returning to Entre Deux Eaux.

From Refuge de la Femma, descend the grassy track to the Chalet de la Rocheure and drop down to cross the stream before continuing along the access road/ track. After a small chapel (Chapelle St Jacques), keep to the road and descend alongside the stream. After 1hr 30min, drop down from the road and cross the Rocheure, then climb the slope to **Refuge Entre Deux Eaux (2hr)**. If you plan to overnight at the refuge (see options below), book in here and leave your rucksack while you continue unburdened into the Leisse valley.

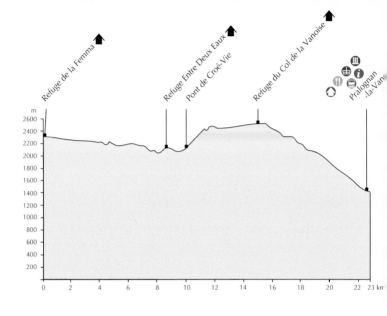

Refuge Entre Deux Eaux (2120m, tel 04 79 05 27 13): This privately owned refuge has 38 dormitory places, a full meals service and kitchen facilities, and is open from early June until late September.

ENTRE DEUX EAUX IN THE 1930S

In 1935 the Scottish climber Janet Adam Smith came to Entre Deux Eaux. She described the refuge as 'a whitewashed stone chalet, rather like a farm-house in the Lakes, long and low rising at one end to a second storey. It was not a CAF refuge... but for years the Richard family, who came up with the cows every summer, had put up climbers or walkers. ...The houses stand on a grassy promontory between the Rocheure and the Leisse, and well above them; the Grande Casse and the Rocher du Col are set back so that the summits can be seen, and the way to the south lies wide open, letting the sun in at all seasons' (*Mountain Holidays*).

Options from Entre Deux Eaux
This is the centre of a trekking wonderland, so if you have time available for further exploration it is a great opportunity. Routes converge from all directions,

The trail descends towards Entre Deux Eaux: the Rocheure valley is to the right and the Leisse valley on the left

and it would be quite possible to spend several days based here without repeating routes. The Grande Motte and Grande Casse rise steeply to the north, whereas the Doron gorge drains spectacularly southwards. The Leisse and Rocheure valleys are wild places with ample options to explore above the refuges at either end of the route, with views across the Doron to the Glaciers de la Vanoise.

For trekkers on the Tour of the Vanoise, the main option is to follow the route from above Pont de Croé-Vie into the Leisse valley and overnight at the Refuge de la Leisse (2hr from Entre Deux Eaux). Or return to the Entre Deux Eaux refuge and the following day continue the trail past Pralognan where there are ample refuges before Péclet-Polset.

From Entre Deux Eaux, to complete the stage, continue north for 1km to the turn to **Pont de Croé-Vie** (2099m, **2hr 15min**). Here, turn left from the path and cross the river, now following the trail described in Stage 9 to the **Col de la Vanoise** (**4hr 30min**) and **Pralognan** (**7hr**).

STAGE 10
Pralognan-la-Vanoise to Refuge de Péclet-Polset

Start	Pralognan-la-Vanoise (1420m)
Finish	Refuge de Péclet-Polset (2474m)
Distance	14km
Ascent	1080m
Descent	30m
Time	5hr
High point	Refuge de Péclet-Polset (2474m)
Facilities	Refuge Le Repoju (1hr 45min) – privately owned refuge;
	Refuge du Roc de la Pêche (2hr 30min) – chalet-refuge;
	Refuge de Péclet-Polset (5hr) – FFCAM refuge

Despite the amount of height gain, this is an undemanding stage which could be achieved in a morning by moderately fast walkers. The first part is mostly along a forest track, but beyond the hamlet of Les Prioux the route leads through open countryside, with a few simple farms seen on either side of the valley and enticing views to the southwest where the twin aiguilles of Péclet and Polset are daubed with ice. As you climb steadily higher, so the valley's headwall becomes more dramatic as it includes the shapely Pointe de l'Échelle, and although the immediate surroundings remain pastoral, the mountains themselves take on an increasingly wild aspect.

The full route from Pralognan to Péclet-Polset is on either a track or a tarmac road, the gradient for the most part generous, with few steep sections to contend with. Yet above and around the refuge, the countryside is refreshingly untamed and challenging. After booking in and taking refreshment there, the temptation to explore will be hard to resist – an attractive tarn is only a few minutes further, and if you have the energy a wild col is a further hour's climb.

Leaving the centre of Pralognan, head upvalley along the main road, which passes Hôtel de la Vanoise and curves right to cross a tributary of the Doron de Chavière river. Immediately over this, bear left along a minor road that takes you past the municipal campsite, Le Chamois. It then bears right where a track eases at first alongside the Isertan campsite, then takes you into it. At crossing tracks, keep ahead to enter forest, with the river thundering in its bed off to your right.

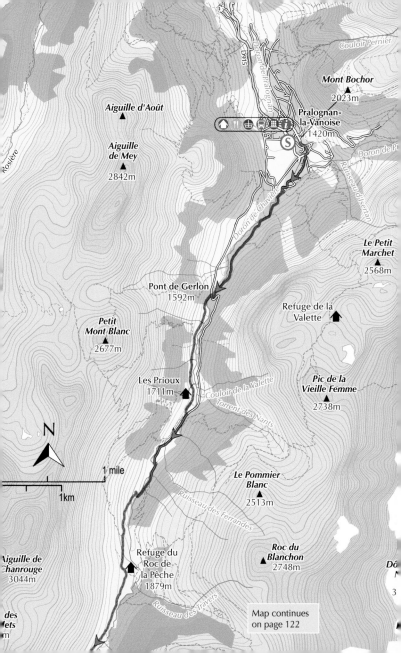

Couloir Pernier

D915

Doron de Pralognan

Mont Bochor
2023m

Aiguille d'Août ▲

Pralognan-
la-Vanoise
1420m

🅢

Doron de Pt

Aiguille
de Mey
2842m

Rosière

Doron de Chavière

Ruisseau d'Isertan

Le Petit
Marchet
2568m ▲

Pont de Gerlon
1592m

Refuge de la
Valette ▲

Petit
Mont Blanc
2677m ▲

Les Prioux
1711m ▲

Couloir de la Valette

Pic de la
Vieille Femme
2738m ▲

Torrent des Nants

N

1 mile

1km

Le Pommier
Blanc
2513m ▲

Ruisseau des Ferrandes

Aiguille de
Chanrouge
3044m ▲

Refuge du
Roc de
la Pêche
1879m ▲

Roc du
Blanchon
2748m ▲

des
ets
m

Ruisseau des Travers

Map continues
on page 122

3

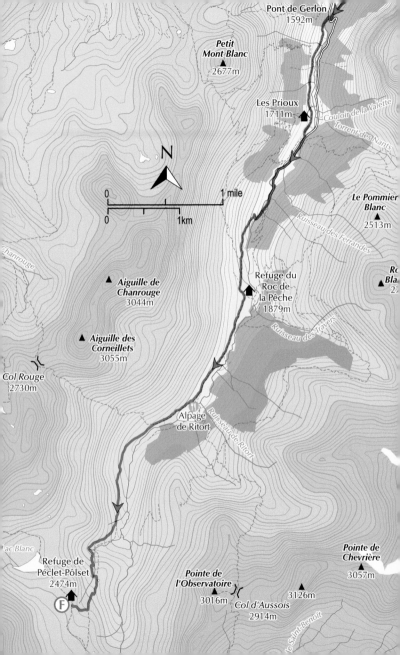

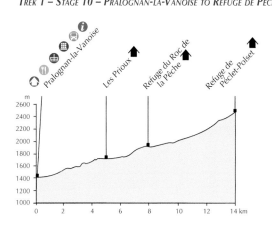

About 20min from Pralognan, pass a turning for the Pont de Chollière. Continue to follow the track signed to Les Prioux. Remain on the track, which rises steadily through the Forêt d'Isertan and eventually spills onto the road by the **Pont de Gerlon** (1592m, **1hr**). Cross the bridge and turn left along another track. Around 100 metres from the bridge, on the left bank of the Doron de Chavière, an outcrop of rocks is popular with local climbers.

The track rises through meadows on the west bank of the river, and before long a path breaks away to make the ascent of the 2677m Petit Mont Blanc, a mountain that is named not for any resemblance to the Monarch of the Alps, but on account of the chalk-white gypsum exposed near the summit. Ignore this option and remain on the track, which leads directly to the stone-built hamlet of **Les Prioux** (1711m, **1hr 45min**).

> **Refuge Le Repoju** (tel 06 83 58 21 73): The Bergerie restaurant offers accommodation in this attractive, privately owned refuge, which has 24 dormitory places and meals provision, and is open from June until late September.

On the south side of the hamlet, join the road and walk along it for approximately 1km as far as a large parking area where the public road ends. Just beyond this, branch right to cross the river on the old stone Pont de la Pêche (1764m). The track winds uphill above a small gorge, climbing quite steeply at times, and on topping a rise you pass the **Refuge du Roc de la Pêche** (**2hr 30min**).

The beautiful Refuge du Roc de la Pêche

Refuge du Roc de la Pêche (1879m, tel 04 79 08 79 75): Standing beside the little chapel of La Motte, and with a splendid view upvalley, the refuge has 60 places in dorms and bedrooms, meals provision, and is open from June until the end of October.

Curving to the right, the track now leads through pastures with impressive views to enjoy towards the head of the valley. Drawing level with the **Alpage de Ritort**, the track forks: you will take the right branch.

The left branch entices with a route across the river to the **Alpage de Ritort**, a cheese-producing summer farm which also has a *buvette* (snacks) – so if you are in need of refreshment, it could be worth the diversion. Beyond the alp buildings, a trail climbs to the **Col d'Aussois** (2914m), used by trekkers tackling the Tour des Glaciers de la Vanoise on the way to Refuge du Fond d'Aussois.

The Péclet-Polset track remains on the west bank, and about 15min later there's another trail junction where the right branch heads for Col Rouge (2731m) and Refuge du Saut. Ignore this and continue ahead, re-entering the national park and maintaining a steady gradient to pass a stone building and a roofless ruin. Beyond these, you curve into a grassy combe, then climb into a wilder, more austere region overlooked by the Pointe de l'Échelle and Aiguille de Polset.

Refuge de Péclet-Polset comes into view as the direct path to the Col de Chavière breaks away from the track. From here, the col may be reached in about 1hr 30min (Refuge de l'Orgère is another 2hr beyond that, or 4hr to Modane). Remain on the track for the final 5min climb to gain the **Refuge de Péclet-Polset (5hr)**.

> **Refuge de Péclet-Polset** (2474m, tel 04 79 08 72 13): Owned by the FFCAM, the refuge has a tragic history, having twice been destroyed by fire. The present building is of modern design and clad in timber with large solar panels. It has 84 dormitory places and full meals provision, with a *gardien* on duty from mid June until mid September. Out of season, 18 places are accessible in the winter room.

LAC BLANC AND COL DU SOUFRE

Of all the huts visited on the Tour of the Vanoise, Péclet-Polset enjoys the wildest aspect. To the south, on the way to Col de Chavière, a stony amphitheatre is dotted with small pools in which iceflows often remain in the early summer. Although these pools are unseen from the refuge, the trail to the col passes them on Stage 11. Big scree fans sweep down from the walling mountains, from which small glaciers and snowfields hang precariously, while their crags and gullies are enough to make a climber's fingers itch.

Northwest of the refuge, Lac Blanc is well worth a visit. Reached in 20min, its milky-blue waters are fed by numerous rivulets draining the Glacier de Gébroulaz, while the twin aiguilles of Péclet and Polset rise from the long line of cliffs behind it. Above the lake, southwest of Pointe des Fonds, the 2817m Col du Soufre offers a challenging route to Refuge du Saut, by which a long day's circuit could be created. This is outlined in the Tour of the Western Vanoise (see Short tour 2), with a return over the summit of the Petit Mont Blanc.

STAGE 11
Refuge de Péclet-Polset to Modane

Start	Refuge de Péclet-Polset (2474m)
Finish	Modane (1050m)
Distance	15km
Ascent	360m
Descent	1790m
Time	5hr 30min
High point	Col de Chavière (2796m)
Facilities	Refuge de l'Orgère (3hr 30min) – PNV refuge; Modane (5hr 30min) – hotels, camping

Col de Chavière is one of the highest passes crossed by any Grande Randonnée route, but when tackled from Refuge de Péclet-Polset on a reasonable summer's day, there are no reasons to feel intimidated by its status. Seen from just above the refuge, the saddle is an obvious one which appears tantalisingly close. Snow inevitably lies in patches on the route to it, and often a steep snow slope may be found on the south side too. But with clear conditions, the col can be reached in about 1hr 30min, although the final steep climb makes a rightful demand for such a pass. However, in poor visibility the route calls for due respect and concentration, while an electrical storm makes this a crossing to avoid.

Descent to Modane offers a choice of two routes, with the trail dividing about 45min below the col. The Orgère route cuts along the east flank of Tête Noire above the Orgère hanging valley, before making a sudden steep descent to Refuge de l'Orgère to join the GR5 for the final downhill trudge through forest shared by the GR55. The alternative and perhaps more direct route along the GR55 bears to the right of the Tête Noire and curves anticlockwise below the southwestern cliff line. The GR55 trail is, perhaps, slightly more demanding than the alternative, while trekkers on the Orgère route are more likely to catch sight of wildlife, and also have an opportunity to stop at the refuge for refreshment or overnight accommodation.

One final thought before decisions are made: it is quite probable that you will need to begin the journey home tomorrow. If so, you may welcome the prospect of a night in a hotel bed with the opportunity to start your journey from Modane in the morning. On the other hand, a return to 'civilisation' may be something you wish to delay as long as possible, in which case a last night may be spent in the sanctity of the mountains; Refuge de l'Orgère is virtually on the route, and you should still have time to descend to Modane after breakfast. The choice is yours!

It is not necessary to return down the track below the Péclet-Polset refuge to join the path to Col de Chavière, for a direct route begins at the hut itself, and is signed. The trail heads west, then curves left (south and southeast) across and through a band of rocks with shrubs growing among them, before joining the main path near a pool. Here you will be greeted by a remarkable forest of elegantly constructed cairns. The way now rises southward, and about 30min from the refuge brings you onto a false col topped by a cairn. The true col can be seen ahead above a wild landscape of slabs, snow patches and ribs of schist. Cairns and paint flashes guide the way up and round the limestone slabs, before you ascend a final sloping ramp of unstable grit (beware of ice, while snow can linger through the summer) which leads directly to the **Col de Chavière** (2796m, **1hr 30min**).

The cairnfield below Col de Chavière has a mystical feel under snow

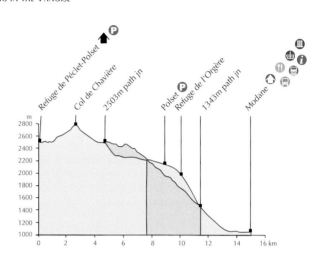

Without question, the **Col de Chavière** is the finest true col on the Tour of the Vanoise, as well as being the highest. It is a narrow saddle in a rocky crest that plunges steeply to north and south. Looking back to the northeast, several of the major Vanoise summits can be seen, as well as the distant, unmistakable snow-crowned Mont Blanc and the dark pyramid of the Aiguille Noire de Peuterey to its right. The view to the south and southeast is no less exciting,

The steep path to the Col de Chavière is made harder by snow in late August

N

0 _____ 1 mile
0 _____ 1km

Lac Blanc

**Refuge de
Péclet-Pôlset**
2474m
Ⓢ

**Pointe de
l'Observatoire**
3016m

*Glacier de
Gébroulaz*

uille
éclet
51m

**Dôme de
Polset**
3497m

**Aiguille
de Polset**
3528m

*Glacier
de la Masse*

**Col de
Chavière**
2796m

**Pointe de
l'Échelle**
3422m

Grand Roc
3316m

*Lac
de la Partie*

*Lac Café
au L'ait*

2503m junction

**Aiguille
Doran**
3040m

**Col de la
Masse**
2922m

**Le Rateau
d'Aussois**
3128m ▲

Ruisseau Noir

Ruisseau de Saint-Bernard

Ruisseau de la Masse

Ruisseau de Povaret

**Tête
Noire**
2675m

GR55 descent

Map continues
on page 130

P

**Refuge
de l'Orgère**
1935m

Lac
de la Partie

Lac Café
au Lait

2503m junction

Aiguille Doran
▲3040m

Col de la Masse
2922m

Le Rateau d'Aussois
3128m ▲

Tête Noire
▲2675m

Ruisseau de Saint-Bernard

Ruisseau Noir

Ruisseau de Povaret

Ruisseau de la Masse

GR55 descent

Refuge de l'Orgère
1935m

Polset

■ Pierre Brune
(ruin)

1343m junction

Ruisseau de Saint-Bernard

Villar
Bou

D215

Loutraz

D1006

L'Arc

Modane

N

0   1 mile

0   1km

eney

L'Arc

D1006

Fourneaux

Quartier Sommeiller

D216

A43

D1006

Ruisseau de

for the highest peaks of the Écrins massif are clearly shown, with the Barre des Écrins catching most attention on account of the glacier draped down its face. Mont Thabor is also visible, as is Monte Viso standing alone far off to the southeast.

Early in the season, a steep snow slope lies below the col; later this slope is composed of scree. Slanting leftward, extra caution is advised until you come to easier ground. The path then winds down various levels, sometimes steeply, before rising a little onto a rock-littered plateau where a signed path cuts left to visit Lac de la Partie. Ignore this and keep ahead for another 5min to reach a major **path junction at 2503m**, about 45min from the col.

For the direct route to Modane, branch right, where the sign indicates 1hr to the Vallon de Polset and 2hr 45min to Modane (see alternative descent via the GR55, described below). For the descent via Orgère, keep left. Whichever you choose, you will very soon reach the end of your Tour of the Vanoise.

Descent to Modane via Orgère

The left-hand path is signed to Orgère in 1hr 30min. It makes a traverse of the left (east) flank of the Tête Noire, descends, then rises again, and continues to the southern end of the Tête Noire spur which overlooks the Arc valley more than 1000m below. Here, the trail suddenly swoops down the steep slope, then twists

The small chapel in Loutraz where the two routes out of Modane come together

through forest before emerging to a car park a short distance from the **Refuge de l'Orgère** (3hr 30min).

> **Refuge de l'Orgère** (1935m, tel 06 51 91 83 71): Fully staffed from June to the end of September, the refuge has 70 dormitory places, full meals service and kitchen facilities. The winter room, which is permanently open, can sleep 14.

For the descent to Modane from the Orgère refuge, take the well-signed GR5 route that drops steeply through woods into Modane in under 2hr. Pass the solitary chalet of **Pierre Brune** in a meadow below L'Orgère, then join the descending GR55 at a **1343m junction** and descend through woods. Recall the stern ascent of the first day (Stage 1) as you glide easily down, but take care of your knees on this last big drop.

Eventually the track curves right to cross the Saint-Bernard stream on a bridge, then left where you soon come out of the trees and onto a road in **Loutraz**. On reaching a minor crossroads by an old chapel, turn left for **Modane** *ville* (the town) or right for Modane *gare* (railway station) (**5hr 30min**).

Alternative descent to Modane via the GR55

The GR55 descent takes a similar time and covers a similar distance to the main descent route. The path descends to the right of the Tête Noire, taking you down through the boulder-strewn pastures of Le Grand Planay, then more steeply into woodland where you contour for a while above the Ruisseau de Saint-Bernard, before dropping into the open meadows to reach the chalets of **Polset** (1840m) where there's a water supply.

Bear left onto a track twisting downhill. A footpath takes you off this track by a house on a bend, below which you cross a road and take another track past the few houses of La Perrière. The descent continues down the steepening slope through forest and brings you to a **junction at 1343m**, about 3hr after crossing Col de Chavière; here, you join the GR5 for the descent to **Modane**, as described above.

TOUR DES GLACIERS
DE LA VANOISE

The Aiguille de la Vanoise looms above the refuge on the Col de la Vanoise (Stage 5)

TREK 2

Tour des Glaciers de la Vanoise

Start/Finish	Pralognan-la-Vanoise
Distance	72km
Time	5 days
High point	Pointe de l'Observatoire (3016m); Col d'Aussois (2914m)
Access	By train and bus to Pralognan via Chambéry and Moûtiers

The Tour des Glaciers de la Vanoise (TdGV) has an older pedigree and is better known to French trekkers than the Tour of the Vanoise (ToV). Making a five-day circuit around the spectacular high mountain region between the Arc valley to the south, the Doron depths to the east and the Pralognan valley to the west, it partly shares its route with the longer ToV. Staying continuously high, it takes in some of the highest cols in the region and provides an opportunity to summit the easy 3000m Pointe de l'Observatoire. At around 72km long, and with over 4000m of ascent (with many opportunities to extend), the TdGV fits comfortably into a one-week trip for those without sufficient time for the whole ToV.

The high mountain dome of the Glacier de la Vanoise is much reduced from its former glory, when it spilled over the lip of the high plateau providing one of the greatest views in France. Old photos in the huts show the extent of the glaciers, and the walk north from the Arpont refuge clearly shows how extensive the glaciation was in the recent past, and how much has been and is being lost.

The route here is described from Pralognan, providing an alternative to the Modane start described in the ToV – although Modane is slightly easier to access by train (see 'How to get there' in the Introduction).

The TdGV is described anticlockwise, but there is no reason why it shouldn't be tackled clockwise – the views are equally impressive and the route just as good to trek. A range of alternatives are available if dictated by a Modane start, bad weather, or other conditions such as heavy early-season snow on the Col d'Aussois.

The first stage involves a stiff climb to the PNV-owned Refuge de la Valette, high above Pralognan, either by a direct unremitting path or (recommended) an exciting trip into the high mountains with cols and cables – a great if slightly stern first day. The refuge is shared with climbers headed to the Dôme de Chasseforêt

The route circuits a broad bowl surrounded by mountains (Stage 4)

– the high point on the Glaciers de la Vanoise – or making the crossing to Refuge de l'Arpont.

On Stage 2, a long traversing path heads south from Refuge de la Valette, staying high above the valley and exploring deep inlets into the mountain barrier. The route then climbs the slopes of the Col d'Aussois. The Pointe de l'Observatoire stands close above, an easy 30min round trip from the col with a few scrambling moves at the top to gain a fine viewpoint. A careful descent leads to the Refuge du Fond d'Aussois, a FFCAM refuge with an enviable view south, or one of the other refuges in the Plan d'Aval basin.

Stage 3 makes a long tour around the Dent Parrachée to Refuge de l'Arpont, while Stage 4 takes you to the iconic Refuge du Col de la Vanoise. From here, the descent to Pralognan (Stage 5) can be made on the same day or after overnighting at Col de la Vanoise.

A Modane start would follow the ToV route from Modane to Orgère, Plan Sec and Arpont (see ToV, Stages 1–3). It could be finished along TdGV Stages 1 and 2, returning to Modane by the ToV route over the Col de Chavière. From Modane, the TdGV would need six days.

STAGE 1
Pralognan-la-Vanoise to
Refuge de la Valette

Start	Pralognan-la-Vanoise (1420m)
Finish	Refuge de la Valette (2554m)
Distance	10km
Ascent	1550m
Descent	420m
Time	5hr
High point	Refuge de la Valette (2554m)
Facilities	Full range of facilities at Pralognan; restaurant at Les Fontanettes, then nothing until Refuge de la Valette

This is a short but hard first day. The route climbs through pleasant woodlands above Pralognan, then follows forest tracks before heading into impressive terrain of rock, passes and some assisted sections (steps and chains). Although steep, nowhere is it really problematic, and after the Col du Grand Marchet, under normal summer conditions most difficulties are past. If there is significant late snow, however, it is advisable to take the direct climb that misses this col.

At the southern end of Pralognan, take the GR55 route uphill to the chapel at Les Bieux, and continue climbing to the cableway, restaurant and parking at **Les Fontanettes** (30min). Head right on a track into woods (the Bois de la Glière). Cross the Doron de Pralognan river and turn left on another track. After a second river crossing (and before a third), find an indistinct path climbing steadily through grass and small bushes. Climb steeply to a **path junction at 1898m** (1hr 30min). (The joining path weaves through the Arcelin valley from the Refuge du Col de la Vanoise. It is an alternative finish route, described at the end of Stage 5, and could also be used by walkers not starting from Pralognan as a route to Refuge de la Valette.)

You are now surrounded by vast rock mountains. Above is the **Petite Aiguille de l'Arcelin** (2650m), and to the south the equally high **Grand Marchet** looms above the onward path.

Turn right at the junction and almost immediately find the first aided section and proceed upwards on paths, metal steps and with cable assistance over the next 500 metres. Nowhere is this particularly difficult, but it is exposed in a couple of places so keep a firm footing and balance, and turn back in case of electrical storms, preferably before any such storm arrives.

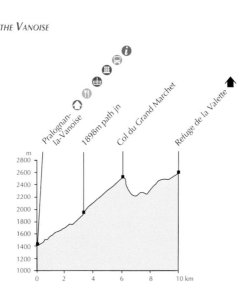

Eventually the path relents, only to steepen again for the final 200m stony climb to the **Col du Grand Marchet** (2490m, **3hr**).

The steep slopes on the far side of the Col du Grand Marchet are a complete break from the rock on the north side

There are very fine views from the **Col du Grand Marchet**, looking back east into the vast rocky buttresses just passed, and ahead into the massive Cirque du Grand Marchet. Two large waterfalls tumble spectacularly from the ridge above.

The descent is over steep grass, dropping 300m to the **Ruisseau d'Isertan**. Cross it and keep left at a junction, passing close beneath the Petit Marchet, which at 2565m is only slightly lower than its cousin, the Grand Marchet. It feels like a lengthy traverse (especially if this is your first day in the high mountains), undulating but steadily climbing from a 2200m low towards the refuge at 2554m, so make the most of opportunities to appreciate the grandeur around.

Pass the path junction where the direct ascent from Pralognan joins (see alternative route described below) and climb through a low ridge, the Roc du Tambour, gaining views across the Lac de la Valette and to the glacial terrain above, before a final short pull to the **Refuge de la Valette (5hr)**.

> **Refuge de la Valette** (2554m, tel 06 65 64 57 36): This is a traditional PNV refuge serving walkers and climbers, for whom it is a jumping-off point for the ascent of the Glaciers de la Vanoise and the crossing to Refuge de l'Arpont. With traditional tent-shaped buildings, it is a warmly inviting spot, with views into the glaciers above, north to the Grande Casse, and south and west to the mountains around Péclet-Polset and the head of the Pralognan valley. The refuge has dormitory space for 44 and is manned from mid June to mid September; there's a full meals service and space for camping.

Alternative ascent direct from Pralognan

This direct ascent involves a steep climb of more than 1100m, which will certainly test the fitness of trekkers newly arrived in the mountains. It begins on the southern outskirts of Pralognan between the two campsites, where a sign indicates the way up through the Forêt d'Isertan. The unrelentingly steep trail finally emerges from the trees on the national park's border on the west flank of the Petit Marchet (2565m). The way continues to climb towards the summit, but then forks right at a junction and swings to the south, easing past the Roc du Tambour, then crossing the Cirque de la Valette to reach the **Refuge de la Valette** (2554m, **4hr**).

STAGE 2
Refuge de la Valette to Refuge du Fond d'Aussois

Start	Refuge de la Valette (2554m)
Finish	Refuge du Fond d'Aussois (2329m)
Distance	20km
Ascent	1230m
Descent	1450m
Time	8hr
High point	Col d'Aussois (2914m); the nearby Pointe de l'Observatoire is at 3016m
Facilities	None until Refuge du Fond d'Aussois; descent into the Pralognan valley is possible in several places, with accommodation and food available at Les Prioux (Refuge Le Repoju) and Refuge du Roc de la Pêche, and refreshments at Alpage de Ritort

A grand stage with everything a mountain day can provide – a peak, passes, glacier views, route-finding challenges and more. It is a long day, so make an early start and carry plenty of supplies as there are none on the route. The first half of the stage, and most of the morning, is a long southbound traverse above 2200m, including a climb into the Cirque du Génépy with dramatic tumbling icefalls high above. The next section is the climb to the Col d'Aussois, which will take over 2hr, perhaps more if you have the energy for the Pointe de l'Observatoire. The descent to the Refuge at Aussois is not long, but it is important to stick to the path as the surrounding rocky terrain descends in a series of slabs and steps.

From the refuge, take either of the descending paths. They soon rejoin and descend to the Chalets des Nants and a stream crossing with a somewhat disappointing 400m initial drop. Pass the descent to the refuge at Les Prioux (unless you need to visit the valley for accommodation) and traverse left and south, undulating through high pastures. Pass a small lake at Chalet Clou (2180m). Where the main (waymarked) path descends, keep straight on along an indistinct path; when the paths rejoin, start to climb into the **Cirque du Génépy**.

Leave the pastures behind and climb into this rocky bowl, with glaciers tumbling high above. Cross the busy stream on a wooden bridge and continue climbing to a high point at around **2460m**, before descending first through rocks and boulders and then across grass again, followed by a final descent to a **2202m path junction** (**4hr**). (The joining path climbs from the Alpage de Ritort; walkers who overnighted at Roc de la Pêche or Les Prioux will rejoin the main route here.)

141

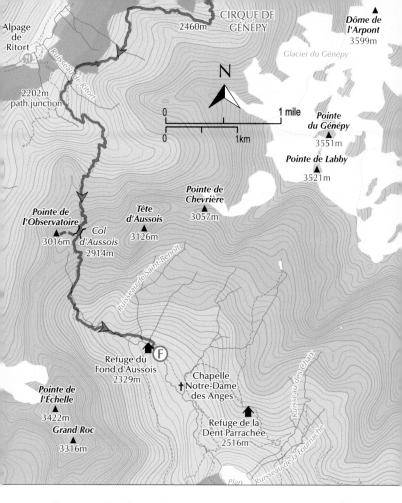

The 700m climb begins almost innocuously, passing pastures and buildings before ascending in earnest. At first, climb the right bank of the Ruisseau de Rosoire (named for the 2776m peak above), then cross and climb ever more steeply alongside a smaller stream. The path is unclear in places, especially if there is early-season snow lingering, but if lost it will soon reappear, with small cairns and intermittent waymarks, so long as you keep climbing. Eventually it relents and you come onto the broad **Col d'Aussois** (2914m, **6hr 30min**).

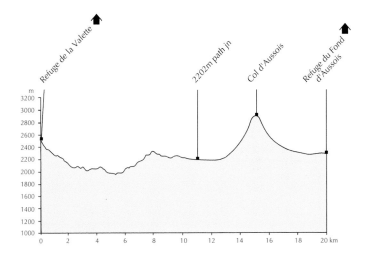

From the **Col d'Aussois** there are views north and south, near and distant. The
Pointe de l'Observatoire (3016m) is near at hand to the west, and is clearly
ascendable. Several paths make the climb, converging into rocky, scrambly

*Looking south from the Pointe de l'Observatoire: the Pointe de l'Échelle and (to the
right) the Col de Chavière*

ground just below the summit. It is only another 100m above the col, roughly a 30min round trip.

From the col, descend initially south through rock steps with sometimes thin waymarking, continuing steeply down. It is important to keep to the route here as the mountainsides are steep and craggy; diverting from the route is not recommended. As the descent unfolds, the options become fewer and fewer. After the long day, it will probably feel endless, but in time the path emerges onto open ground and the hut is visible for the last kilometre. **Refuge du Fond d'Aussois** is reached in around 1hr 30min from the col (**8hr**).

> **Refuge du Fond d'Aussois** (2329m, tel 04 79 20 39 83): The refuge has accommodation for 52 and a *gardien* in summer, providing a full meals service and the possibility of camping. Looking out over a bowl of pastureland, the hut is well sited with excellent views to the south.

Looking down on the Refuge du Fond d'Aussois. At this point most of the descent has been done

STAGE 3
Refuge du Fond d'Aussois to
Refuge de l'Arpont

Start	Refuge du Fond d'Aussois (2329m)
Finish	Refuge de l'Arpont (2309m)
Distance	20km
Ascent	860m
Descent	880m
Time	6hr 30min
High point	Above La Turra (2462m)
Facilities	Refuges (Fournache, Dent Parrachée, Plan Sec, Montana) in the first hour of the stage, then no facilities until Refuge de l'Arpont

This is a tremendous walk that joins with the third stage of the Tour of the Vanoise. After an initial amble through level meadows, the route dips towards the Plan d'Amont and d'Aval lakes and then climbs, passing Refuge de Plan Sec (far too soon for lunch, and maybe too soon even for coffee). It then crosses the Dent Parrachée–Pointe de Bellecôte ridge at La Turra, before contouring back into the central Vanoise region high above the Doron de Termignon. The route to Arpont can seem longer, with continual ups and downs, but the fine refuge at the end of the stage is well worth the effort.

With flowers and peaks, the walking is excellent

Take the path south from the Aussois refuge, crossing a level plateau speckled with farm buildings, a small chapel (**Notre-Dame des Anges**) and almost certainly sheep or cows. After 30min, drop down to a path junction (2248m) and turn left, with views of the lakes below, passing in front of **Refuge de la Fournache**. (Refuge de la Dent Parrachée is 30min off route from here.) From this point on, you are on the GR5 through to Arpont. Cross pastures and streams before rising gradually towards **Refuge de Plan Sec** (**1hr**), which stands a short climb above the main track.

Drop down below ski lifts and pass above the **Chalet-Hôtel Le Montana** to enter a vast combe, passing high pastures and farms. The broad track then turns into a path that climbs through an eroded section, potentially exposed to stonefall but following a well-engineered path, rising to the 2363m viewpoint of **La Turra** (**2hr 15min**). The view to the south embraces the Mont Cenis range and the south side of the Maurienne, with the villages of the Arc valley looking tiny, over 1000m below.

Beyond La Turra, climb on wide zigzags to a high point (2462m). The trail turns north, passing the wide slopes of La Dent Parrachée (3697m). Continuously between 2200m and 2450m, the trail is always clear, passing paths rising from the Termignon valley at **La Loza** (**3hr 30min**) and **Montafia** (**5hr**). The refuge eventually comes into view across a valley with at least three streams to cross, after which a final pull brings you to the rebuilt **Refuge de l'Arpont** (**6hr 30min**).

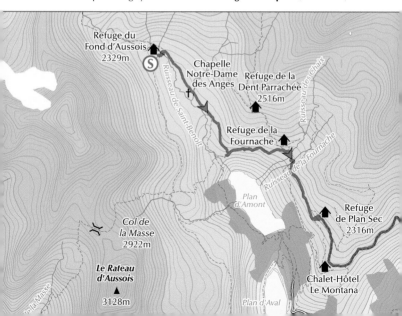

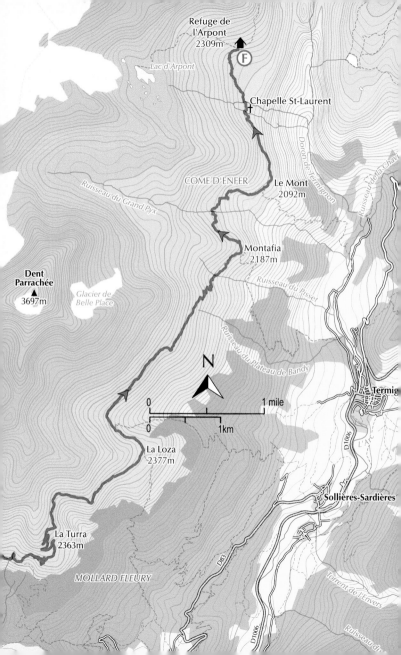

Refuge de
l'Arpont
2309m
(F)

Lac d'Arpont

Chapelle St-Laurent

Doron de Termignon

COME D'ENFER
Le Mont
2092m

Ruisseau du Grand Pyx

Montafia
2187m

Ruisseau du Pisset

Dent
Parrachée
3697m

Glacier de
Belle Place

Ruisseau du Plateau de Bandy

N

Ruisseau de la Chavi

Termig

L'Arc

0   1 mile

0   1km

La Loza
2377m

Sollières-Sardières

La Turra
2363m

D83

MOLLARD FLEURY

Torrent de l'Envers

D1006

Ruisseau du

D1006

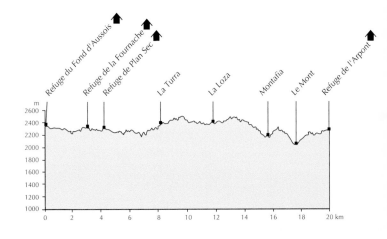

Refuge de l'Arpont (2309m, tel 09 82 12 42 13): With 94 dormitory places plus overnight camping, the refuge also provides full meals provision, kitchen facilities, and a resident *gardien* from early June to late September.

Mountains to the south are visible above the Doron de Termignon

STAGE 4
Refuge de l'Arpont to
Refuge du Col de la Vanoise

Start	Refuge de l'Arpont (2309m)
Finish	Refuge du Col de la Vanoise (2517m)
Distance	14km
Ascent	660m
Descent	450m
Time	5hr
High point	Above Refuge de l'Arpont after the initial climb (2560m)
Facilities	None on the route, but Refuge Entre Deux Eaux is seen 300m below the trail; a diversion there would add around 1hr 20min to the walk

A fairly short day, but it provides great walking throughout. Firstly, the northward progress of Stage 3 continues, past grazing chamois and with the tremendous depth of the Doron de Termignon far below, before bringing you to the attractive Lacs des Lozières. This is an ideal place to slow down and appreciate the glacier on the Dôme de Chasseforêt, as well as the rocky buttresses of the Pointe de la Réchasse. The route passes beneath these, providing opportunities to admire the complex junction of valleys around Entre Deux Eaux, which can be visited if you wish to inspect both streams at close hand. Views of the Rocheure and Leisse valleys, traversed on the Tour of the Vanoise, show clearly the great walking potential of the eastern Vanoise. The route then enters the approach valley to the Col de la Vanoise, tightly crowded between the Grande Casse and the Pointe de la Réchasse, before climbing gently to the refuge, spectacularly sited on a broad col surrounded by mountains.

Take the GR5 north from Arpont, with an initial climb of nearly 200m, then descend slabs (awkward if icy or snow-covered) to the **Ruisseau de Miribel**; it may be difficult to retain dry feet when crossing this wide stream early in the season. Climb over another ridge and follow the path along a moraine, before descending stone and moraine to a stream crossing (Ruisseau de la Letta) after which you turn to the **Lacs des Lozières**, an area of great beauty and somewhere to linger (**2hr**).

Aiguille de
la Vanoise
2796m

Refuge du
Col de la
Vanoise
2517m

(F)

Lac Rond

Ruisseau de la Vanoise

■ blockhouse

memorial ·

Vallon d

Pont
Croé-
2099

Grande Aiguille
de l'Arcelin
2759m

Pointe de
la Réchasse
3212m

*Glacier de la
Roche Ferran*

Roche Ferran
3099m

*Lac de la
Roche Ferran*

Refuge
d'Entre Deux Ea
2120m

Draie des frés
2329m
path junction

La Para ■

Refuge du
Plan du Lac
2364m

*Lacs des
Lozières*

Ruisseau de la Letta

Ruisseau du Plan de Grassan

Ruisseau de Mribel

Doron de Termignon

*Lac de
Chassefôrét*

N

0 _____ 1 mile

0 _____ 1km

Refuge de
l'Arpont
2309m

(S)

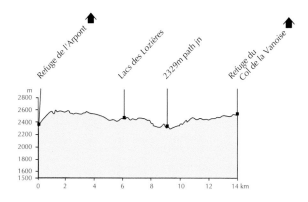

Climb steadily again, with views into the deep Doron gorge and ahead towards the Vallon de la Rocheure, before dropping to a **path junction at 2329m**. The GR5 descends towards Entre Deux Eaux, but we take the path left (north), traversing the rock-strewn slopes of the Pointe de la Réchasse. The Leisse valley comes into view and you join the GR55, the trail which has climbed from the Pont de Croé-Vie.

Pass a **memorial** to two army officers and a wartime **blockhouse**, and enter the almost level valley, initially keeping to the north side before drifting to the south. After passing two tarns, there is a final short pull to the **Refuge du Col de la Vanoise (5hr)**.

Refuge du Col de la Vanoise (2517m, tel 04 79 08 25 23): This large and very popular refuge is owned by the FFCAM. It has 129 dormitory places, full meals service and self-catering facilities, and is staffed from early March until the end of September. Views are tremendous and dominated by the Grande Casse, below which lies yet another lake, Lac Long. Marmots abound almost everywhere.

STAGE 5
*Refuge du Col de la Vanoise to
Pralognan-la-Vanoise*

Start	Refuge du Col de la Vanoise (2517m)
Finish	Pralognan-la-Vanoise (1420m)
Distance	8km
Ascent	Negligible
Descent	1100m
Time	2hr 30min
High point	Col de la Vanoise (2517m)
Facilities	Refuge at Les Barmettes (1hr 15min); restaurant at Les Fontanettes (2hr)

A short stage to finish, and it's all downhill. Although it could be tacked on to the previous stage, that would miss a final night in the high mountains. The Aiguille de la Vanoise, although a modest height for this region, dominates the first part of the descent, before the iconic and much-photographed causeway across Lac des Vaches. The descent shifts from rock to grass, and Les Barmettes refuge is passed about halfway down. A ski lift may be running, which could speed the descent, but the walk through woods is always attractive, passing the restaurant at Les Fontanettes before taking a secluded path direct to Pralognan. An alternative, less direct and quieter finish via the Arcelin valley is also described.

Take the GR55 onward route, passing above **Lac Long**; high above on the left is the Aiguille de la Vanoise, a popular rock climb. Keep descending through moraine and the remains of glaciers, passing the photogenic steps across **Lac des Vaches** (**30min**) and continuing to **Refuge Les Barmettes** (2010m, **1hr 15min**). Descend through woods above ski areas and pass **Les Fontanettes** restaurant and parking area, last seen on Stage 1, before following the GR55's final descent into **Pralognan**, turning right for the town centre (**2hr 30min**).

Alternative route to Pralognan or Refuge de la Valette
If you started the Tour des Glaciers in Modane, or elsewhere in the Arc valley, there is an option not to descend to Pralognan but to cross more directly to the

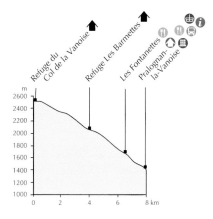

Valette refuge. This route could also be used as an alternative finish by walkers returning to Pralognan.

Instead of taking the GR55 from Refuge du Col de la Vanoise, head west from the refuge, passing **Lac des Assiettes** and the ruined Chalets de l'Arcelin. (From here, it is possible to make a 1km detour to the 2297m summit of Le Moriond, with its great views to the high mountains.)

The long and stony descent to Pralognan around the Aiguille de la Vanoise

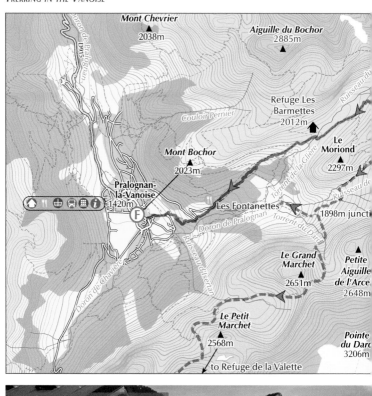

Pralognan is a pleasant low-key resort

To continue, descend alongside the **Ruisseau de l'Arcelin** (a potentially slippery descent, so take care) to a **path junction at 1898m**, which is reached in slightly less than 1hr 30min from Refuge du Col de la Vanoise.

To return to Pralognan, turn right at the 1898m junction and descend steeply to a forest track. Turn left and follow the track to a bridge; cross the bridge to join the main descent route near **Les Fontanettes**, before joining the GR55 down to **Pralognan**.

Walkers heading for Refuge de la Valette turn left at the 1898m junction and continue across the slabs and assisted sections as described in Stage 1, crossing the Col du Grand Marchet and passing beneath the Petit Marchet to reach Refuge de la Valette.

SHORT TOURS
IN THE VANOISE

*Looking over Lac Blanc to the Col du Soufre; the route
climbs the right-hand side of the col (Short tour 2)*

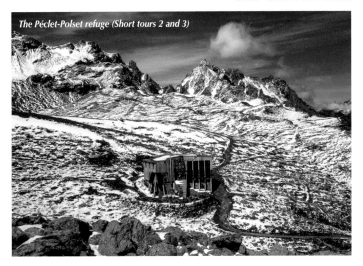
The Péclet-Polset refuge (Short tours 2 and 3)

In addition to the main Tour of the Vanoise (ToV) and Tour des Glaciers de la Vanoise (TdGV), a number of shorter treks can be made in the district. Some of these are publicised locally, with leaflets published by the Parc National de la Vanoise (PNV). There is also the Traverse of the Vanoise, following the route of the GR5 and GR55; this is another very fine hut-to-hut tour demanding slightly fewer days than the full ToV and TdGV circuits.

Three of these tours are outlined below. While full route descriptions are not given, the information and overview maps provided should prove sufficient to enable you to follow the routes on the Carte de Randonnée 1:50,000 *A3 Vanoise* map. A number of sections overlap with the ToV and TdGV, so further details may be found in the relevant stages of those routes.

SHORT TOUR 1
Tour of the Eastern Vanoise
(Tour de Méan Martin et du Grand Roc Noir)

Start/Finish	Bonneval-sur-Arc
Distance	64km
Time	4 days
High point	Col des Fours (2976m); Col de la Rocheure (2911m)
Access	By bus from Modane, which is on the high-speed TGV rail link with Paris via Chambéry
Note	Refuge du Plan du Lac could be used as an alternative start; it is reached by bus from Termignon in the Maurienne valley, between Modane and Bonneval

The Pointe de Méan Martin and the Grand Roc Noir are high points on the long ridge of 3000m peaks that wall the Haute-Maurienne between the valley of the Doron de Termignon and Col de l'Iseran. This four-day tour makes an elongated circuit of that wall, which falls on its north side into the Vallon de la Rocheure. Three PNV refuges are used for overnight accommodation.

The route involves substantial ascent and descent, and two passes in excess of 2900m have to be crossed; since both passes are likely to have snow cover until late June at the earliest, walkers are advised not to attempt the route too early in the season. The paths are good and straightforward in good weather, but if visibility is poor, navigation could be difficult. As such, this tour is best tackled by trekkers with sufficient experience of these conditions.

Stage 1 – Bonneval-sur-Arc to Refuge du Vallonbrun
For the first stage of the tour, the route to Refuge du Vallonbrun reverses Stage 6 of the Tour of the Vanoise (ToV), heading downvalley to Le Villaron and Bessans, and continuing through La Chalp to the hamlet of Le Collet on the Col de la Madeleine. Thus far, the trek is gentle and undemanding, but from Le Collet the path climbs abruptly up the steep north flank of the valley, finally emerging by the Chapelle St-Antoine a short stroll from the Refuge du Vallonbrun (2272m, tel 04 79 05 93 93). Reached in 5hr from Bonneval, this charming PNV refuge has

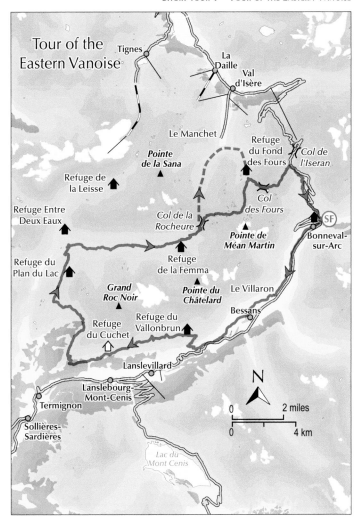

27 dormitory places, plus camping space, a full meals service and a *gardien* from June to mid September.

Reflection of the Grande Motte in the tarn at Plan du Lac (photo: Kev Reynolds)

Stage 2 – Refuge du Vallonbrun to Refuge du Plan du Lac

With 18.5km and a steep uphill section to face, this 6hr stage can seem quite demanding. Once again it reverses a section of the ToV (Stage 5), which means following the route of the GR5 all the way. Rising gently at the start, the path then undulates southwestward along the steep mountainside, until reaching the unmanned Refuge du Cuchet (2160m, tel 04 79 62 30 54), a PNV refuge with 24 dormitory places and kitchen facilities.

Leaving the refuge, the path drops steeply to a track, which then contours along the hillside and into forest. At a junction marked Pré Vaillant, leave the track for a signed path which labours uphill among trees, climbing more than 300m before turning a spur at the Chalets de la Turra. Cross through a rocky gap at La Turra de Termignon, and head across broad pastureland with a few alp farms dotted about the landscape. The path spills onto a track which leads eventually to a parking area known as Bellecombe in the valley of the Doron de Termignon. A path now rises onto an open grassland in which lies a beautiful lake, and shortly after passing this you arrive at the Refuge du Plan du Lac (2364m, tel 04 79 20 50 85). With 42 dormitory places and full meals provision, this PNV refuge is manned from June to the end of September.

Stage 3 – Refuge du Plan du Lac to Refuge du Fond des Fours

Having turned the western end of the Méan Martin/Roc Noir ridge system on Stage 2, the route now trends northeastward, and on leaving Plan du Lac a trail angles across the lower slopes of the Pointe de Lanserlia and turns into the Vallon de la Rocheure. Two-thirds of the way through this lovely valley, you come to the PNV's Refuge de la Femma (2352m, tel 04 79 05 45 40). It has 64 dormitory places, camping space, and a *gardien* from mid June until late September.

The way now climbs to the **Col de la Rocheure** (2911m) and flanks eastward, initially marked by substantial cairns in wild terrain. It contours below Pointe Sud des Lorès, then turns a spur and makes a northerly descent to Refuge du Fond des Fours (2537m, tel 06 03 54 50 55) about 6hr after leaving Plan du Lac. Facing Pointe de Méan Martin to the south, this timber-built PNV refuge is similar in style to the Femma hut. It has 42 dormitory places, full meals provision, and a *gardien* from mid June to mid September.

Bad weather alternative
Only take the direct route outlined from Col de la Rocheure to the Fond des Fours refuge if conditions are good; otherwise descend from the Col de la Rocheure heading northwest into the Vallon du Pisset, where you come to a roadhead at **Le Manchet**, then curve right and climb through the Bézin valley to gain the refuge. (See ToV Stage 8A and Stage 7 alternative, in reverse.)

Stage 4 – Refuge du Fond des Fours to Bonneval-sur-Arc
To conclude the tour, return a short distance along the route by which you approached the refuge, with the Pointe de Méan Martin directly ahead, then bear left for a steady 400m ascent to the **Col des Fours** (2976m). Lying midway between Pélaou Blanc and Pointe des Fours, the col makes a splendid vantage point, but given sufficient time and energy a diversion to the summit of Pointe des Fours (3072m) is recommended for a much more expansive view. The route cuts along the west side of the ridge, and there should be no technical difficulties to the ascent, which gains less than 100m in height.

On the east side of the col, descend left of a lake, below which there's a patch of névé to wander through (noted on the Carte de Randonnée 1:50,000 *A3 Vanoise* map as the Ancien Glacier de la Jave). In summer there should be plenty of marks showing the way, and at the foot of the slope you come to the GR5 near Pont de la Neige on the Iseran road. Turn right and follow the GR5 trail down through the Lenta gorge, and via Vallon de la Lenta as far as Bonneval-sur-Arc (in effect, reversing part of ToV Stage 7).

SHORT TOUR 2
Tour of the Western Vanoise

Start/Finish	Pralognan-la-Vanoise
Distance	48km
Time	3 days
High point	Col du Soufre (2817m); Petit Mont Blanc (2677m)
Access	By train and bus to Pralognan via Chambéry and Moûtiers

This short tour of the infrequently visited western national park begins easily with a walk along the Doron de Chavière valley to the Péclet-Polset refuge, before striking boldly into little-walked terrain to the north. Passing Lac Blanc and the high point at the remote Col du Soufre, it makes a long descent alongside the Gébroulaz glacier to a privately owned refuge, before again striking into a little-walked landscape and making its way to another remote refuge and the beautiful Lacs Merlet. The last day takes in a high viewpoint before dropping back into Pralognan's valley, where a fourth day could easily be passed if desired. The ski resorts of Les Trois Vallées are hidden behind the ridgeline to the west, so they do not intrude on this wild country walk.

Stage 1 – Pralognan-la-Vanoise to Refuge de Péclet-Polset
The walk starts with a gentle climb into the Doron de Chavière valley south of Pralognan. Refreshments are possible at several spots along the route – Les Prioux, Roc de la Pêche, Ritort – with most of the climb coming towards the end of the stage. Strong walkers will cover this stage in a morning, but the beauty of the valley and the peaks surrounding it should encourage a relaxed approach. Used by trekkers following the Tour of the Vanoise, Refuge de Péclet-Polset (2474m, tel 04 79 08 72 13) has 84 places, meals provision and a *gardien* from mid June to mid September.

Stage 2 – Refuge de Péclet-Polset to Refuge des Lacs Merlet
After the gentle amble of Stage 1, this is a totally different day, remote and high. From the refuge, climb past the much-visited **Lac Blanc** and then onwards to

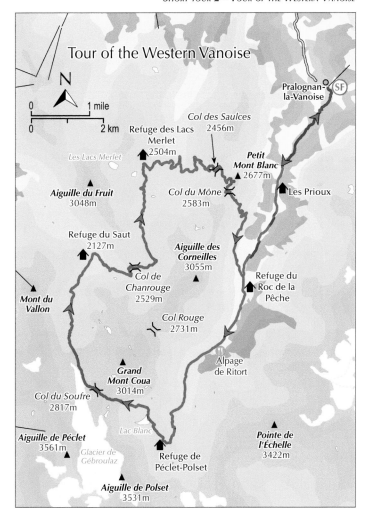

Tour of the Western Vanoise

Pralognan-la-Vanoise SF

Col des Saulces 2456m

Refuge des Lacs Merlet 2504m

Les Lacs Merlet

Petit Mont Blanc 2677m

Les Prioux

Aiguille du Fruit 3048m

Col du Mône 2583m

Refuge du Saut 2127m

Aiguille des Corneilles 3055m

Refuge du Roc de la Pêche

Col de Chanrouge 2529m

Mont du Vallon

Col Rouge 2731m

Grand Mont Coua 3014m

Alpage de Ritort

Col du Soufre 2817m

Lac Blanc

Aiguille de Péclet 3561m

Glacier de Gébroulaz

Refuge de Péclet-Polset

Pointe de l'Échelle 3422m

Aiguille de Polset 3531m

the less-frequented **Col du Soufre** (2817m). The path is steep and it crosses the remains of the Glacier de Gébroulaz, which drapes the north flank of the twin Péclet and Polset peaks. The descending path is occasionally unclear and may initially be affected by the impact of the receding glacier, but it always stays firmly on the glacier's right bank before crossing its stream at 2400m and descending to the remote, privately owned Refuge du Saut (2127m, tel 09 74 77 60 38). Reached in 3hr after leaving Péclet-Polset, the refuge has 25 dormitory places when manned, usually mid June to mid September.

From Refuge du Saut, cross the river and climb southeast alongside the Ruisseau to Chanrouge before a turn north and a steep climb brings you to the **Col de Chanrouge** (2529m). Onwards, descend gradually through pastures, eventually coming to the tiny Refuge des Lacs Merlet (2504m, tel 04 79 06 56 76). With just 14 places, booking is advisable in this remote spot. Facilities are limited, but the refuge has a resident *gardien* from mid June to mid September. The Lacs Merlet are close by.

Stage 3 – Refuge des Lacs Merlet to Pralognan-la Vanoise

This stage crosses little-visited country high above the resort of Courchevel (far below, and not seen). Pass the site of the former Grand Plan refuge (2320m) and then make a twisting climb to another Lac Blanc and the **Col des Saulces** (2456m).

Petit Mont Blanc (2677m) can be climbed from the north, west or south – all ascents are steep but on good paths. The path on the west flank is probably easiest and disguises the outlook until you reach the very top, where there are great views to the Grande Casse and Mont Blanc in the north. To descend, take the west flank again, or the south ridge, and come to the **Col du Mône** (2583m).

The view over the Pralognan valley and the Grande Casse from the Petit Mont Blanc peak

The Glacier de Gébroulaz and the Péclet-Polset peaks at its head

Descend steeply to the valley, where an overnight is possible in one of two refuges, putting off the end of the trek until tomorrow. Refuge du Roc de la Pêche (1879m, tel 04 79 08 79 75) has 60 places and meals provision, and is open from June until the end of October. Less than 1hr downvalley, the privately owned Refuge Le Repoju (1711m, tel 06 83 58 21 73) in the hamlet of Les Prioux offers 24 places and meals provision, and is open from June until late September. Overnighting at one or the other makes a tempting alternative to continuing to Pralognan, which is only a couple of hours away and can be reached the same day.

SHORT TOUR 3

Traverse of the Vanoise via the GR5 and GR55

Start	Landry
Finish	Modane
Distance	86km
Time	5 days
High point	Col de Chavière (2796m)
Access	Landry has a railway station on the Chambéry to Bourg-St-Maurice line; Modane is also linked with Chambéry (and Paris) by high-speed TGV rail link

By combining the GR5 with the GR55, this splendid north-to-south crossing of the Vanoise district can be achieved in five days. Unlike the previously described tours, this is a linear route, one of the highlights of the 674km Grande Traversée des Alpes, the full extent of which will take most walkers at least four weeks to complete (see *The GR5 Trail* by Paddy Dillon, Appendix D).

Beginning in Landry, in the lower Isère valley, the first day takes you past a string of villages up into more remote countryside on the fringe of the national park. After crossing Col du Palet next day, the GR5 drops to Tignes le Lac, where the traverse then heads south to join the GR55 all the way to Modane, sharing stages adopted by the scenic Tour of the Vanoise.

Stage 1 – Landry to Refuge d'Entre-le-Lac

For a first day's walk, this stage of around 6hr 30min will be quite long enough. It begins on a road but soon deserts this for the trail of the GR5, which mostly avoids tarmac except where it visits one or more of the villages built on what is descriptively known as Le Versant du Soleil (the Hillside of the Sun). Above the last of these villages, about 2–3hr from Landry, you come to the PNV-owned Refuge de Rosuel (1556m, tel 04 57 37 65 94). With 64 dormitory places and full meals provision, the refuge is open with a *gardien* from June to the end of September.

The way climbs on, passing through scrub with waterfalls dashing the northern slopes, then turns to the south where the scenery becomes more enticingly

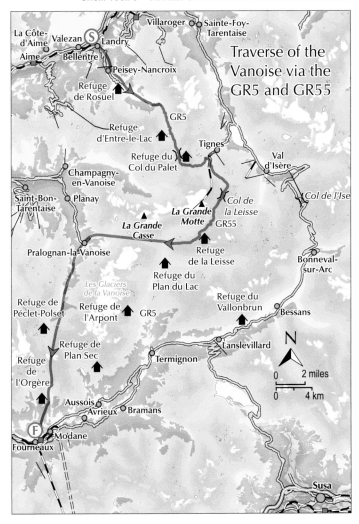

Traverse of the
Vanoise via the
GR5 and GR55

remote. All the left-hand side of the valley is within the national park, and after
the path forks at 2050m the GR5 actually traces the boundary line. At the fork,

take the right branch, which stays close to the Ponturin stream and follows it to Lac de la Plagne, beyond which stands Refuge d'Entre-le-Lac (2145m, tel 04 79 04 20 44). Privately owned, it has 44 dormitory places, full meals provision, and is open from mid June to mid September.

Stage 2 – Refuge d'Entre-le-Lac to Refuge de la Leisse

A more demanding stage than that of the first day, this route is around 7hr long, with two passes to cross. It begins by rejoining the GR5 in a little under 30min, then climbs – steeply at times – to Lac du Grattaleu which lies below Refuge du Col du Palet (tel 04 79 07 91 47). Another PNV refuge, this one has 47 dormitory places, plus space for camping, full meals service and a *gardien* from mid June to mid September.

The Col du Palet (2652m) is just 5–10min above the refuge, and provides excellent views of the nearby Grande Motte and Grande Casse glaciers. The col also marks a national park boundary, which you leave as you descend towards Tignes le Lac. In 45min from the col, the trail enters the Combe des Militaires, where there's a junction. Since it's not necessary to go into Tignes (unless you need refreshments or supplies), you can branch right at the junction and cut across to Val Claret. Here, you join the GR55 for the climb to **Col de la Leisse** (2729m), re-entering the national park on the way.

On the south side of the col, the trail descends through a stony trough of a valley below the east and south flanks of La Grande Motte, before arriving at the

On the GR5 finish, looking across to the mountains south of the Arc valley

Refuge de la Leisse (2487m, tel 09 72 40 03 23, out of season tel 06 15 44 33 68). Another PNV refuge, it has 32 dormitory places, space for camping, full meals provision, kitchen facilities, and a *gardien* from mid June to mid September.

Stage 3 – Refuge de la Leisse to Pralognan-la-Vanoise
On joining the GR55 at Val Claret on yesterday's stage, the Traverse of the Vanoise effectively hitched onto the route of the Tour of the Vanoise (ToV). Today's trek to Pralognan follows ToV Stage 9, a 6hr route which first descends through the lovely Vallon de la Leisse to Pont de Croé-Vie. (There is an option here to break away on the GR5 for a more southerly route to Modane, following the first few stages of the ToV in reverse.)

After Pont de Croé-Vie, our route stays with the GR55 and climbs to the Col de la Vanoise, with its substantial refuge and extraordinary views of La Grande Casse, Pointe de la Grande Glière, the Pointes de l'Épéna, Aiguille de l'Épéna, huge moraines and small lakes. Over the col, a broad trail swoops down to Lac des Vaches at the foot of the Aiguille de la Vanoise, then continues the descent past the privately owned Refuge Les Barmettes and on down to Pralognan in the valley of the Doron de Chavière.

Stage 4 – Pralognan-la-Vanoise to Refuge de Péclet-Polset
This very fine 5hr valley walk traces ToV Stage 10, and although there's more than 1000m of height to gain over a distance of about 14km, it's not an overly demanding trek. But as you progress through the valley heading southwest, so the high mountain scenery expands and grows more dramatic, making it a visually enriching walk. And on arrival at the refuge, the rugged landscape has a quality of wild enchantment, with the snow- and ice-draped Pointe de l'Échelle dominating the view to the left of Col de Chavière. For once, it's a relief to have time to explore the surroundings of Refuge de Péclet-Polset (2474m, tel 04 79 08 72 13), a modern FFCAM refuge. With 84 dormitory places and full meals provision, the refuge is staffed from mid June until mid September.

Stage 5 – Refuge de Péclet-Polset to Modane
At 2796m, **Col de Chavière** is the high point of the traverse, a narrow saddle in a rocky crest with far-reaching views to both north and south. Reached in 1hr or so from Refuge de Péclet-Polset, it's a great place to sit (weather permitting) and absorb the wild beauty of the Alps. The descent to Modane, however, is long and tiring and, in places, very steep, although it does pass through more fine scenery. The full route is described in ToV Stage 11, and makes a fitting finale to a memorable five-day trek.

APPENDIX A
Useful contacts

If calling France from another country, use the international access code for that country (from the UK, the code is 00) followed by the country code for France (33), then drop the initial 0 of the area code.

Information
French Tourist Office
www.france.fr/fr

Parc National de la Vanoise (PNV)
www.vanoise-parcnational.fr/fr

Fédération Française de la Randonnée Pédestre (FFRP)
www.ffrandonnee.fr

Map suppliers
Cordee
tel 01455 611185
www.cordee.co.uk

The Map Shop
15 High Street
Upton-upon-Severn
Worcs
WR8 0HJ
tel 01684 593146
www.themapshop.co.uk

Stanfords
7 Mercer Walk
Covent Garden
London
WC2H 9FA
tel 020 7836 1321
www.stanfords.co.uk

Specialist mountain activities insurance
Austrian Alpine Club (UK)
tel 01929 556870
www.aacuk.org.uk
(*AAC members only. Membership carries automatic accident and rescue insurance, plus reciprocal rights reductions in FFCAM refuges.*)

British Mountaineering Council
tel 0161 445 6111
www.thebmc.co.uk
(*BMC members only*)

Snowcard Insurance Services Ltd
tel 01702 427273
www.snowcard.co.uk

Flights

Airlines
British Airways
www.britishairways.com

EasyJet
www.easyjet.com

Ryanair
www.ryanair.com

Search/Comparison websites
Cheapflights.com
(*for schedules and low-price offers*)
www.cheapflights.com

Ebookers
(*for low fares on scheduled flights*)
www.ebookers.com

Expedia
(*for discount fares and daily deals*)
www.expedia.co.uk

Skyscanner
www.skyscanner.co.in

Rail travel
Rail Europe
(*rail journeys within Europe*)
www.raileurope.com

Seat 61
(*general information on European train travel*)
www.seat61.com

SNCF
(*French train travel*)
www.sncf.com/fr (*timetables*)
www.oui.sncf (*bookings*)

Trainline
(*rail journeys within Europe*)
www.thetrainline.com

Weather forecasts
Météo-France
https://meteofrance.com/
meteo-montagne

Mountain-Forecast.com
www.mountain-forecast.com

Emergencies
Emergency services
tel 112

PGHM (Peloton de Gendarmerie de Haute Montagne)
(*French mountain rescue*)
tel 04 79 05 18 04 (Modane)
tel 04 79 07 01 10 (Bourg-St-Maurice)

APPENDIX B
Accommodation

The following list details accommodation providers along the routes described in this guide. The type of accommodation on offer, opening season and website are given, where known. Many websites are in French only, but web browsers often offer a translation service. Further details can be obtained from the various tourist offices.

Refuges – in alphabetical order
(42d = 42 dormitory places; d&b = dorms & bedrooms)

Refuge de l'Arpont
94d + camping; early June to late Sept
tel 09 82 12 42 13
https://refuge-arpont.vanoise.com

Refuge Les Barmettes
27d + camping; mid June to mid Sept
tel 04 79 08 75 64
www.lesbarmettes-refuge.com

Chalet-Refuge Bonneval-sur-Arc
15d; all year; there may be restrictions due to COVID-19 (at times it has been unmanned and in summer 2021 occupancy was limited to 10)
tel 04 78 42 09 17
online reservations only via website
https://chaletbonnevalsurarc.ffcam.fr

Refuge du Col de la Vanoise
129d; early March to end Sept
tel 04 79 08 25 23
https://refugecoldelavanoise.ffcam.fr

Refuge du Col du Palet
47d + camping; mid June to mid Sept
tel 04 79 07 91 47
https://refuge-coldupalet.vanoise.com

Refuge du Cuchet
24d; self-catering only; July to end Aug
tel 04 79 62 30 54
www.maurienne-tourisme.com/hebergement/refuge-du-cuchet-185120

Refuge de la Dent Parrachée
42d + camping; late May to late Sept
tel 04 79 20 32 87
https://refugeladentparrachee.ffcam.fr
www.dentparrachee.refuges-vanoise.com

Refuge Entre Deux Eaux
38d; early June to late Sept
tel 04 79 05 27 13
www.refuges-vanoise.com

Refuge d'Entre-le-Lac
44d; mid June to mid Sept
tel 04 79 04 20 44
https://refugeentrelelac.wixsite.com/savoie

Refuge de la Femma
64d + camping; mid June to late Sept
tel 04 79 05 45 40
https://refuge-femma.vanoise.com

Refuge du Fond d'Aussois
52d + camping; June to end Sept
tel 04 79 20 39 83
https://refugefonddaussois.ffcam.fr
www.fondaussois.refuges-vanoise.com

Refuge du Fond des Fours
42d; mid June to mid Sept
tel 06 03 54 50 55
https://refuge-fonddesfours.vanoise.com

Refuge de la Fournache
34d + camping; mid June to mid Sept
tel 06 09 38 72 38
www.fournache.refuges-vanoise.com

Refuge des Lacs Merlet
14d; mid June to mid Sept
tel 04 79 06 56 76
www.vanoise-parcnational.
fr/fr/hebergement-collectif/
refuge-refuge-des-lacs-merlet-courchevel

Refuge de la Leisse
32d + camping; mid June to mid Sept
tel 09 72 40 03 23
tel 06 15 44 33 68 (out of season)
https://refuge-leisse.vanoise.com

Chalet-Hôtel Le Montana
60d&b + camping; early July to mid
Aug
tel 04 79 20 31 47
https://chalet-montana.com

Refuge de l'Orgère
70d; end May to end Sept
tel 06 51 91 83 71 or 09 72 19 24 07
https://refuge-orgere.vanoise.com

Refuge de Péclet-Polset
84d; mid June to mid Sept
tel 04 79 08 72 13
https://refugepecletpolset.ffcam.fr

Refuge du Plan du Lac
42d; June to end Sept
tel 04 79 20 50 85
https://refuge-plandulac.vanoise.com

Refuge de Plan Sec
52d + camping; mid June to mid Sept
tel 04 79 20 31 31
https://refuges-vanoise.com

Refuge Le Repoju
24d; June to late Sept
tel 06 83 58 21 73
www.refuge-repoju.com

Refuge du Roc de la Pêche
60d&b; June to end Oct
tel 04 79 08 79 75
www.lerocdelapeche.com

Refuge de Rosuel
64d; June to end Sept
tel 04 57 37 65 94
https://refuge-rosuel.vanoise.com

Refuge du Saut
25d; mid June to mid Sept
tel 09 74 77 60 38
https://refuges-vanoise.com

Refuge de la Valette
44d + camping; mid June to mid Sept
tel 06 65 64 57 36
https://refuge-valette.vanoise.com

Refuge du Vallonbrun
27d + camping; June to mid Sept
tel 04 79 05 93 93
https://refuge-vallonbrun.vanoise.com

Hotels, gîtes and campsites

The following accommodation options are listed under the town or village in which they are located. Please note that the list is by no means comprehensive. Further information can be obtained from the tourist offices, which are also included here.

Bessans
Tourist office
Rue de la Maison Morte
73480 Bessans
tel 04 79 05 96 52
https://www.haute-maurienne-vanoise.
com

Gîte d'étape Le Petit Bonheur
tel 04 79 05 06 71
www.lepetitbonheur-bessans.fr

Gîte de la Bâtisse
Le Villaron, Bessans
tel 04 79 83 14 51
www.gitedelabatisse.com

Hôtel Le Grand Fond
tel 04 79 05 83 05

Hôtel La Vanoise
tel 04 79 05 96 79
http://hotel-vanoise.com

Campsites
Camping de l'Illaz
tel 06 45 89 02 32
https://www.camping-bessans.com

Camping La Grange du Traverole
tel 06 87 58 18 51
www.lagrangedutraverole.com

Bonneval-sur-Arc
Tourist office
Résidence Ciamarella
73480 Bonneval-sur-Arc
tel 04 79 05 95 95
https://www.haute-maurienne-vanoise.
com

Gîte d'étape Auberge d'Oul
tel 04 79 05 87 99
www.auberge-oul.com/fr/index.php

Hôtel Le Glacier des Évettes
tel 04 79 05 94 06
www.hotel-bonnevalsurarc.com

Val d'Isère
Tourist office
Place Jacques Mouflier
73150 Val d'Isère
tel 04 79 06 06 60
www.valdisere.com/en

Hôtel Les Crêtes Blanches
tel 04 79 06 05 45
https://www.cretes-blanches.fr

Camping
Camping Les Richardes
tel 06 95 36 20 40
http://campinglesrichardes.free.fr

Landry
Tourist office
tel 04 79 07 94 28
www.peisey-vallandry.com

Hôtel L'Alpin
tel 04 79 55 33 00
www.hotel-lalpin.com/fr

Hôtel Émeraude
tel 04 79 07 94 46
www.hotel-emeraude.com

Modane
Tourist office
Place Sommeiller
73500 Modane
tel 04 79 05 26 67
https://www.haute-maurienne-vanoise.
com

Hôtel de la Gare
tel 04 79 83 26 19
www.hoteldelagare-modane.com

Hôtel Les Voyageurs
tel 04 79 05 01 39
www.lesvoyageurshotel.fr

Hôtel Le Perce-Neige
tel 04 79 05 00 50
www.hotel-leperceneige.com

Hôtel Le Commerce
tel 04 79 05 20 98
www.hotel-le-commerce.net

Camping
Camping La Vanoise
tel 04 79 05 21 39
http://camping-la-vanoise.simplesite.
com

Pralognan-la-Vanoise
Tourist office
290 avenue de Chasseforêt
73710 Pralognan-la-Vanoise
tel 04 79 08 79 08
www.pralognan.com

Hôtel Les Airelles
tel 04 79 08 70 32
www.hotel-les-airelles.fr

Epicéa Lodge
tel 04 79 08 73 11
www.epicealodge.com

Hôtel Le Grand Bec
tel 04 79 08 71 10
www.hoteldugrandbec.fr

Hôtel La Vallée Blanche
tel 04 79 08 70 74

Hôtel de la Vanoise
tel 04 79 08 70 34
www.hoteldelavanoise.fr

Camping
Alpes Lodges (Camping Isertan)
tel 04 79 08 75 24
http://camping-alpeslodges.com

Camping Municipal Le Chamois
tel 06 59 46 45 34
www.pralognan.com/
campinglechamois-3.html

Tignes le Lac
Tourist office
73320 Tignes
tel 04 79 40 04 40
https://en.tignes.net

APPENDIX C

French–English glossary

On the trail

French	English
abri	shelter
activités de plein air	outdoor activities
aiguille	needle-like peak
alpiniste	mountaineer
ampoule	blister
arête	ridge
balisage	waymark
barrage	dam
bergerie	shepherd's hut, sheepfold
bois	woodland
buvette	snack bar, café
cairn	cairn
chemin	footpath
chute de pierres	rockfall
club alpin	alpine club
col	pass
colline	hill
combe	small valley
couloir	steep gully
crête	crest, ridge
croix	cross
dessous	lower
dessus	upper
éboulis	scree
facile	easy
ferme	farmhouse
fontaine	spring (of water)
forêt	forest

French	English
lac	lake
mauvais pas	bad (or difficult) step
montagne	mountain
névé	snowfield
pâturage	pasture
plaine/plagne/plan	plain, plateau
plateau	plateau
pont	bridge
réservoir	reservoir
rivière	river
ruisseau	stream
sentier	footpath
sommet	summit
source	spring (of water)
torrent	mountain stream
val/vallée/vallon	valley

Directions

French	English
droite	right (direction)
est	east
gauche	left (direction)
nord	north
ouest	west
sud	south
tout droit	straight ahead

Equipment

French	English
boussole	compass
carte	map
carte pédestre	walking map
chaussures de montagne	boots
corde	rope
piolet	ice axe
sac à dos	rucksack
sac à viande	sleeping bag liner
sac de couchage	sleeping bag

Weather and time

French	English
aujourd'hui	today
beau temps	good weather
brouillard	fog
chaud	warm
demain	tomorrow
éclair	lightning
ensoleillé	sunny
froid	cold
glace	ice
heure	hour
météo	weather forecast
neige	snow
nuage	cloud

French	English
orage	storm
orageux	stormy
pluie	rain
soleil	sun
tempête	storm
tonnerre	thunder
vent	wind

Accommodation

French	English
bain	bath
chalet-refuge	mountain inn
chambre	bedroom
chambre d'hôte	B&B
complet	full
couchette	bunk bed
demi-pension	half board
dortoir	dormitory
douche	shower
gîte d'étape	walkers' hostel
libre	free
liste d'hôtels	hotel list
logement	accommodation
occupé	occupied
pension complète	full board
refuge	mountain hut

Mealtimes

French	English
carte	menu
déjeuner	lunch
dîner	dinner
petit déjeuner	breakfast
pique-nique	lunch packet, picnic
repas	meal

Food and drink

French	English
ail	garlic
beurre	butter
bière	beer
boissons	drinks
boissons chaudes	hot drinks
café/café au lait	black coffee/ coffee with milk
carte des vins	wine list
casse-croûte	snack
champi-gnons	mushrooms
charcuterie	cured meats served cold
chips	crisps
chocolat	chocolate
chocolat chaud	hot chocolate
confiture	jam

French	English
croque madame	toasted ham-and-cheese sandwich with egg
croque monsieur	as above, but without the egg
croûte au fromage	hot cheese-and-garlic bread
crudités	chopped raw vegetables, salad
fondue savoyard	cheese fondue (heated at the table and eaten with cubed bread)
eau	water
frites	chips, French fries
fromage	cheese
gâteau	cake
haricots	beans
hors-d'œuvres	starters
jambon	ham (boiled)
jambon cru	cured sliced ham
jambon fumé	smoked ham
jus d'orange	orange juice
légumes	vegetables

French	English
lentilles	lentils
miel	honey
œuf	egg
omelette nature	plain omelette
pain	bread
pâté	pâté
pâtes	pasta
pâtisserie	pastries, cakes
plat du jour	dish of the day
plats chauds	hot dishes
plats froids	cold dishes
poisson	fish
poivre	pepper
pomme	apple
pomme de terre	potato
potage	soup
poulet	chicken
riz	rice
saucisson	sausage
sel	salt
sucre	sugar
thé	tea
thé au lait	tea with milk
thon	tuna
tisane	herbal tea
truite	trout

French	English
viande	meat
vin blanc/ rouge	white/red wine
volailles	poultry

Transport

French	English
autobus/autocar	bus
chemin de fer	railway
horaire	timetable
navette	shuttle bus
téléphérique	cable car
télésiège	chairlift
TGV (train à grande vitesse)	high-speed train

Towns and villages

French	English
alimentation	grocery
arrêt (d'autobus)	(bus) stop
banque	bank
boucher	butcher
boulangerie	bakery
chapelle	chapel
échange	exchange (currency)
église	church
épicerie	grocery
fermé	closed

French	English
gare	railway station
gare routière	bus station
magasin	shop
office de tourisme	tourist office
ouvert	open
pharmacie	chemist
renseignements	information
supermarché	supermarket
syndicat d'initiative	tourist office
ville	town

Animals

French	English
aigle	eagle
bouquetin	ibex
chamois	chamois
marmotte	marmot

Colours and sizes

French	English
blanc/blanche	white
bleu/bleue	blue
grand/grande	big
jaune	yellow
noir/noire	black
petit/petite	small
rouge	red
vert/verte	green

Greetings

French	English
Bonjour, monsieur/ madame	Good morning, sir/ madam
Bonsoir	Good evening
Bonjour	Hello
Salut, Jean	Hi, John
Ça va, Pierre?	How's it going, Peter?
Comment allez-vous?	How are you?
Bonne chance!	Good luck!
Bonne nuit	Goodnight
Au revoir	Goodbye

Useful phrases at the refuge

French	English
S'il vous plaît	Please
Merci	Thank you
Excusez-moi	Excuse me
Où est le gardien?	Where is the hut warden?
Avez-vous un lit libre pour ce soir/demain, s'il vous plaît?	Have you a bedfree for tonight/tomor-row, please?

French	English
Mon nom est… *J'ai réservé une place par téléphone*	My name is… I made a reservation by telephone
Quel est le prix par nuit?	How much does it cost per night?
Puis-je camper ici?	Can I camp here?
Puis-je avoir un repas/demi-pension/le petit déjeuner/une bière?	Can I have a meal/half board/breakfast/a beer?
À quelle heure est le dîner/petit déjeuner?	What time is dinner/breakfast?
Où est la salle à manger?	Where is the dining room?
Où sont les douches/toilettes?	Where are the showers/toilets?

French	English
L'addition, s'il vous plaît	Could I have the bill, please?
Quel temps va-t-il faire aujourd'hui?	What's the weather going to be like today?
Un moment, s'il vous plaît	Just a moment, please
D'accord	OK
Je ne comprends pas	I do not understand
Parlez-vous anglais?	Do you speak English?

Emergencies

French	English
Au secours!	Help!
coup de soleil	sunstroke
dangereux	dangerous

APPENDIX D

Bibliography

Surprisingly little has been written in English about the Graian Alps – the proper name for the Vanoise region – so the literature is sparse. A few accounts of mountaineering ascents appear in various journals, and an occasional article of interest to walkers appears in the outdoor press, but there is little in comparison with certain other Alpine districts. However, the following books contain material that is both informative and entertaining for anyone planning a visit to this delightful range.

Dillon, Paddy: *The GR5 Trail* (Cicerone Press, 3rd edn, 2016) – an excellent guide to a classic long-distance route which passes through the region on its way from Lake Geneva to Nice. Accurate and inspiring, with many fine photographs.

Fairbairn, Helen, and Gareth McCormack et al: *Walking in the Alps* (Lonely Planet, 2004) – includes a section devoted to the Tour des Glaciers de la Vanoise.

Henderson, Paul: *Vanoise Ski Touring* (Cicerone Press, 2003) – making the most of winter in these mountains, this guide describes 11 ski tours and a selection of the best ski-mountaineering ascents.

Hodges, Andy: *Mountain Adventures in the Maurienne* (Cicerone Press, 2011) – as the title suggests, this is a multi-activity guide offering routes for walkers, trekkers, via ferrata enthusiasts and mountain bikers.

Lieberman, Marcia R: *The Outdoor Traveler's Guide: The Alps* (Stewart, Tabori and Chang, New York, 1991) – lavishly illustrated with colour photographs by Tim Thompson, this is a good primer by an American devotee of the Alps. A brief chapter is given to the Vanoise National Park.

Lieberman, Marcia R: *Walking the Alpine Parks of France and Northwest Italy* (The Mountaineers, Washington, 1994; distributed in the UK by Cordee) – contains a chapter on the Vanoise National Park and describes a number of day-walks and a few short tours.

Michelin Green Guide: French Alps (Michelin, 8th edn, 2020) – a standard tourist guide covering the French Alps, from Lake Geneva to the Alpes Maritimes, it includes several items of interest to visitors to the Vanoise region.

Reynolds, Kev: *Walking in the Alps* (Cicerone Press, 2nd edn, 2005; reprinted 2017) – describes the whole Alpine chain, from the Alpes Maritimes to the Julian Alps of Slovenia, and includes a section devoted to the Graian Alps, with both the Tour of the Vanoise and the Tour des Glaciers de la Vanoise described.

Reynolds, Kev: *Trekking in the Alps* (Cicerone Press, 2011) – a large-format guide describing a selection of 20 of the best multi-day treks in the Alps; includes the Tour of the Vanoise.

Reynolds, Kev: *100 Hut Walks in the Alps* (Cicerone Press, 3rd edn, 2014; reprinted 2018) – day-walks to huts in most Alpine regions, including the Vanoise.

Reynolds, Kev: *The Mountain Hut Book* (Cicerone Press, 2018) – all you could ever want to know about mountain huts and the hutting experience in the Alps.

Smith, Janet Adam: *Mountain Holidays* (JM Dent, 1946) – in this minor classic of mountain literature the author describes the delights of pre-war active holidays spent in Scotland and the Alps, with several references to the Vanoise region.

Out of print

Akitt, JW: *Walking in the Tarentaise and Beaufortain Alps* (Cicerone Press, 1995) – a guidebook for walkers with details of 53 day-walks and four mostly short tours in these neighbouring mountain areas. Useful for trekkers planning a return to explore the region further.

Reynolds, Kev: *Alpine Points of View* (Cicerone Press, 2004) – a collection of 100 colour photographs and essays describing the rich diversity of the Alpine chain, including several landscapes experienced by walkers on the Tour of the Vanoise.

Unsworth, Walt (editor): *Classic Walks of the World* (Oxford Illustrated Press, 1985) – a large-format book that has a chapter by Martin Collins describing the GR55 Traverse of the Vanoise from Landry to Modane – nicely illustrated in colour and black and white.

NOTES

NOTES

DOWNLOAD THE ROUTES
IN GPX FORMAT

All the routes in this guide are available for download from:

www.cicerone.co.uk/863/GPX

as standard format GPX files. You should be able to load them into most online GPX systems and mobile devices, whether GPS or smartphone. You may need to convert the file into your preferred format using a conversion programme such as gpsvisualizer.com or one of the many other such websites and programmes.

When you follow this link, you will be asked for your email address and where you purchased the guidebook, and have the option to subscribe to the Cicerone e-newsletter.

www.cicerone.co.uk

LISTING OF CICERONE GUIDES

BRITISH ISLES CHALLENGES, COLLECTIONS AND ACTIVITIES
The Big Rounds
The Book of the Bivvy
The Book of the Bothy
The C2C Cycle Route
The Mountains of England and Wales:
    Vol 1 Wales
    Vol 2 England
The National Trails
Walking The End to End Trail
Cycling Land's End to John o' Groats

SCOTLAND
Ben Nevis and Glen Coe
Cycle Touring in Northern Scotland
Cycling in the Hebrides
Great Mountain Days in Scotland
Mountain Biking in Southern and Central Scotland
Mountain Biking in West and North West Scotland
Not the West Highland Way
Scotland
Scotland's Best Small Mountains
Scotland's Mountain Ridges
Skye's Cuillin Ridge Traverse
The Borders Abbeys Way
The Great Glen Way
The Great Glen Way Map Booklet
The Hebridean Way
The Hebrides
The Isle of Mull
The Isle of Skye
The Skye Trail
The Southern Upland Way
The Speyside Way
The Speyside Way Map Booklet
The West Highland Way
The West Highland Way Map Booklet
Walking Ben Lawers, Rannoch and Atholl
Walking in the Cairngorms
Walking in the Pentland Hills
Walking in the Scottish Borders
Walking in the Southern Uplands
Walking in Torridon
Walking Loch Lomond and the Trossachs
Walking on Arran
Walking on Harris and Lewis
Walking on Jura, Islay and Colonsay
Walking on Rum and the Small Isles
Walking on the Orkney and Shetland Isles
Walking on Uist and Barra
Walking the Cape Wrath Trail

Walking the Corbetts
    Vol 1 South of the Great Glen
    Vol 2 North of the Great Glen
Walking the Galloway Hills
Walking the Munros
    Vol 1 – Southern, Central and Western Highlands
    Vol 2 – Northern Highlands and the Cairngorms
Winter Climbs Ben Nevis and Glen Coe
Winter Climbs in the Cairngorms

NORTHERN ENGLAND TRAILS
Hadrian's Wall Path
Hadrian's Wall Path Map Booklet
The Coast to Coast Walk
The Coast to Coast Walk Map Booklet
The Pennine Way
The Pennine Way Map Booklet
Walking the Dales Way
Walking the Dales Way Map Booklet
Walking the Tour of the Lake District

NORTH EAST ENGLAND, YORKSHIRE DALES AND PENNINES
Cycling in the Yorkshire Dales
Great Mountain Days in the Pennines
Mountain Biking in the Yorkshire Dales
St Oswald's Way and St Cuthbert's Way
The Cleveland Way and the Yorkshire Wolds Way
The Cleveland Way Map Booklet
The North York Moors
The Reivers Way
The Teesdale Way
Trail and Fell Running in the Yorkshire Dales
Walking in County Durham
Walking in Northumberland
Walking in the North Pennines
Walking in the Yorkshire Dales: North and East
Walking in the Yorkshire Dales: South and West

NORTH WEST ENGLAND AND THE ISLE OF MAN
Cycling the Pennine Bridleway
Cycling the Reivers Route
Cycling the Way of the Roses
Hadrian's Cycleway
Isle of Man Coastal Path
The Lancashire Cycleway

The Lune Valley and Howgills
Walking in Cumbria's Eden Valley
Walking in Lancashire
Walking in the Forest of Bowland and Pendle
Walking on the Isle of Man
Walking on the West Pennine Moors
Walks in Silverdale and Arnside

LAKE DISTRICT
Cycling in the Lake District
Great Mountain Days in the Lake District
Joss Naylor's Lakes, Meres and Waters of the Lake District
Lake District Winter Climbs
Lake District: High Level and Fell Walks
Lake District: Low Level and Lake Walks
Mountain Biking in the Lake District
Outdoor Adventures with Children – Lake District
Scrambles in the Lake District – North
Scrambles in the Lake District – South
The Cumbria Way
Trail and Fell Running in the Lake District
Walking the Lake District Fells:
    Borrowdale
    Buttermere
    Coniston
    Keswick
    Langdale
    Mardale and the Far East
    Patterdale
    Wasdale

DERBYSHIRE, PEAK DISTRICT AND MIDLANDS
Cycling in the Peak District
Dark Peak Walks
Scrambles in the Dark Peak
Walking in Derbyshire
Walking in the Peak District – White Peak East
Walking in the Peak District – White Peak West

SOUTHERN ENGLAND
20 Classic Sportive Rides in South East England
20 Classic Sportive Rides in South West England
Cycling in the Cotswolds
Mountain Biking on the North Downs
Mountain Biking on the South Downs
Suffolk Coast and Heath Walks

The Cotswold Way
The Cotswold Way Map Booklet
The Great Stones Way
The Kennet and Avon Canal
The Lea Valley Walk
The North Downs Way
The North Downs Way Map Booklet
The Peddars Way and Norfolk
  Coast path
The Pilgrims' Way
The Ridgeway National Trail
The Ridgeway National Trail
  Map Booklet
The South Downs Way
The South Downs Way Map Booklet
The Thames Path
The Thames Path Map Booklet
The Two Moors Way
The Two Moors Way Map Booklet
Walking Hampshire's Test Way
Walking in Cornwall
Walking in Essex
Walking in Kent
Walking in London
Walking in Norfolk
Walking in the Chilterns
Walking in the Cotswolds
Walking in the Isles of Scilly
Walking in the New Forest
Walking in the North Wessex Downs
Walking on Dartmoor
Walking on Guernsey
Walking on Jersey
Walking on the Isle of Wight
Walking the Jurassic Coast
Walking the South West Coast Path
Walking the South West Coast Path
  Map Booklets:
  Vol 1: Minehead to St Ives
  Vol 2: St Ives to Plymouth
  Vol 3: Plymouth to Poole
Walks in the South Downs
  National Park

WALES AND WELSH BORDERS

Cycle Touring in Wales
Cycling Lon Las Cymru
Glyndwr's Way
Great Mountain Days in Snowdonia
Hillwalking in Shropshire
Hillwalking in Wales – Vols 1&2
Mountain Walking in Snowdonia
Offa's Dyke Path
Offa's Dyke Path Map Booklet
Ridges of Snowdonia
Scrambles in Snowdonia
Snowdonia: 30 Low-level and easy
  walks – North
Snowdonia: 30 Low-level and easy
  walks – South
The Cambrian Way
The Ceredigion and Snowdonia
  Coast Paths
The Pembrokeshire Coast Path

Pembrokeshire Coast Path
  Map Booklet
The Severn Way
The Snowdonia Way
The Wales Coast Path
The Wye Valley Walk
Walking in Carmarthenshire
Walking in Pembrokeshire
Walking in the Forest of Dean
Walking in the Wye Valley
Walking on Gower
Walking on the Brecon Beacons
Walking the Shropshire Way

INTERNATIONAL CHALLENGES, COLLECTIONS AND ACTIVITIES

Canyoning in the Alps
Europe's High Points

AFRICA

Kilimanjaro
The High Atlas
Walks and Scrambles in the Moroccan
  Anti-Atlas
Walking in the Drakensberg

ALPS CROSS-BORDER ROUTES

100 Hut Walks in the Alps
Alpine Ski Mountaineering
  Vol 1 – Western Alps
  Vol 2 – Central and Eastern Alps
Chamonix to Zermatt
The Karnischer Hohenweg
The Tour of the Bernina
Tour of Monte Rosa
Tour of the Matterhorn
Trail Running – Chamonix and the
  Mont Blanc region
Trekking in the Alps
Trekking in the Silvretta and
  Ratikon Alps
Trekking Munich to Venice
Trekking the Tour of Mont Blanc
Walking in the Alps

PYRENEES AND FRANCE/SPAIN CROSS-BORDER ROUTES

Shorter Treks in the Pyrenees
The GR10 Trail
The GR11 Trail
The Pyrenean Haute Route
The Pyrenees
Walks and Climbs in the Pyrenees

AUSTRIA

Innsbruck Mountain Adventures
The Adlerweg
Trekking in Austria's Hohe Tauern
Trekking in the Stubai Alps
Trekking in the Zillertal Alps
Walking in Austria
Walking in the Salzkammergut: the
  Austrian Lake District

EASTERN EUROPE

The Danube Cycleway Vol 2
The High Tatras
The Mountains of Romania
Walking in Bulgaria's National Parks
Walking in Hungary

FRANCE, BELGIUM AND LUXEMBOURG

Chamonix Mountain Adventures
Cycle Touring in France
Cycling London to Paris
Cycling the Canal de la Garonne
Cycling the Canal du Midi
Mont Blanc Walks
Mountain Adventures in
  the Maurienne
Short Treks on Corsica
The GR20 Corsica
The GR5 Trail
The GR5 Trail – Benelux and Lorraine
The GR5 Trail – Vosges and Jura
The Grand Traverse of the
  Massif Central
The Loire Cycle Route
The Moselle Cycle Route
The River Rhone Cycle Route
The Way of St James – Le Puy to the
  Pyrenees
Tour of the Queyras
Trekking in the Vanoise
Trekking the Cathar Way
Trekking the Robert Louis
  Stevenson Trail
Vanoise Ski Touring
Via Ferratas of the French Alps
Walking in Provence – East
Walking in Provence – West
Walking in the Ardennes
Walking in the Auvergne
Walking in the Briançonnais
Walking in the Dordogne
Walking in the Haute Savoie: North
Walking in the Haute Savoie: South
Walking on Corsica

GERMANY

Hiking and Cycling in the
  Black Forest
The Danube Cycleway Vol 1
The Rhine Cycle Route
The Westweg
Walking in the Bavarian Alps

IRELAND

The Wild Atlantic Way and
  Western Ireland
Walking the Wicklow Way

ITALY

Italy's Sibillini National Park
Shorter Walks in the Dolomites

For full information on all our guides, books and eBooks, visit our website:
www.cicerone.co.uk

CICERONE

Trust Cicerone to guide your next adventure,
wherever it may be around the world...

Discover guides for hiking, mountain walking, backpacking,
trekking, trail running, cycling and mountain biking, ski touring,
climbing and scrambling in Britain, Europe and worldwide.

Connect with Cicerone online and find inspiration.

- buy books and ebooks
- articles, advice and trip reports
- podcasts and live events
- GPX files and updates
- regular newsletter

cicerone.co.uk